COMPOST EVERYTHING

CASTALIA HOUSE

NON-FICTION
A History of Strategy: From Sun Tzu to William S. Lind by Martin van Creveld
Equality: The Impossible Quest by Martin van Creveld
On War: The Collected Columns of William S. Lind 2003-2009 by William S. Lind
Four Generations of Modern War by William S. Lind
Transhuman and Subhuman: Essays on Science Fiction and Awful Truth by John c.
    Wright

MILITARY SCIENCE FICTION
Riding the Red Horse Vol. 1 ed. Tom Kratman and Vox Day
There Will Be War Vol. I ed. Jerry Pournelle
There Will Be War Vol. II ed. Jerry Pournelle

SCIENCE FICTION
Awake in the Night Land by John C. Wright
City Beyond Time: Tales of the Fall of Metachronopolis by John C. Wright
Somewhither by John C. Wright
Big Boys Don't Cry by Tom Kratman
The Stars Came Back by Rolf Nelson
Hyperspace Demons by Jonathan Moeller
On a Starry Night by Tedd Roberts
Do Buddhas Dream of Enlightened Sheep by Josh M. Young
QUANTUM MORTIS A Man Disrupted by Steve Rzasa and Vox Day
QUANTUM MORTIS Gravity Kills by Steve Rzasa and Vox Day
QUANTUM MORTIS A Mind Programmed by Jeff Sutton, Jean Sutton, and Vox Day
Victoria: A Novel of Fourth Generation War by Thomas Hobbes

FANTASY
One Bright Star to Guide Them by John C. Wright
The Book of Feasts & Seasons by John C. Wright
A Magic Broken by Vox Day
A Throne of Bones by Vox Day
The Gladiator's Song by Vox Day
The Wardog's Coin by Vox Day
The Last Witchking by Vox Day
Summa Elvetica: A Casuistry of the Elvish Controversy by Vox Day
The Altar of Hate by Vox Day
The War in Heaven by Theodore Beale
The World in Shadow by Theodore Beale
The Wrath of Angels by Theodore Beale

COMPOST EVERYTHING

The Good Guide to Extreme Composting

David
The
Good

Compost Everything: The Good Guide to Extreme Composting

by David the Good

Published by Castalia House
Kouvola, Finland
www.castaliahouse.com

Cover Design: JartStar
Editor: Vox Day

To Rachel.

Thanks for taking out the compost while I was writing.

Contents

Introduction

Over the decades, various priests and prophets of composting have attempted to set in stone a list of rules defining exactly how a gardener should make compost.

This book throws out those rules.

You can compost a ridiculous variety of materials in a wide range of outrageous ways.

Food for your soil is everywhere. Unfortunately, this potential fertility often hits the trash rather than completing the nutrient loop and making its way back into the ground.

If you hate the trash you create, this book is for you.

If you're a rule-breaker and a visionary, this book is for you.

If you're ready to grow the best gardens you've ever grown, this book is for you.

It's time to break the chains and petty rules.

It's time to ***COMPOST EVERYTHING!***

1. Thirty-Two Reasons to Compost

Before we get into the nitty-gritty, let's take a quick look at some reasons *why* composting is so valuable.

1. Composting saves money.

When you make compost, you potentially save money on water, fertilizer, and trash service.

2. Composting releases your inner fairy godmother.

Mice into horses, pumpkins into carriages, and kitchen scraps into black gold... Bippity-boppity boo-yah!

3. Compost makes your plants happier.

Gardeners like happy plants... and plants that get compost are definitely happy.

4. Composting reduces household waste.

Composting keeps your food waste out of the waste stream. You can compost paper, cardboard, and anything organic. That means fewer bags of trash and less smell from your trash cans.

5. Composting saves fuel.

Imagine how much gas could be saved if everyone quit chucking their food and yard "waste" and started composting instead. Just doing that on one property makes a difference. The less that needs to be hauled around, the better.

6. Composting keeps you from throwing away fertility.

Throwing away potential soil fertility is an utter waste, yet people do it all the time.

7. Compost made at home saves energy.

Homemade compost keeps you from traveling (which consumes energy) to buy factory-made fertilizer (which takes energy to produce) made from mined minerals (which take energy to mine), which are then packaged (which also requires energy and additional materials—usually plastic). If you're already gardening organically, making compost also keeps you from traveling to buy organic amendments, which still require collecting, bagging, and packaging.

8. Composting is enjoyable.

Whether you make layers or just throw it in a pile to rot, creating compost is fun. Think of it as a big rotten food fight.

9. Compost made at home is safer than compost purchased at a store.

Purchased compost can contain almost anything from pesticides and herbicides to weed seeds to heavy metals.

10. Compost builds soil.

This goes without saying, but it's still a wonderful thing.

11. Compost saves water.

Adding compost to your soil significantly increases water retention, which means you'll have to water less.

12. Compost feeds the microorganisms in your soil.

Although microscopic life is easy to forget, it's also a vital part of your soil's health. It is a great big web of life with many checks and balances. Adding compost keeps this web happy and active.

13. Compost makes your crops taste better.

More nutrition in the soil equates to more nutrition in your vegetables, which results in more flavor! You can literally taste the difference between vegetables grown in poor soil and vegetables grown in nutrient-rich soil.

14. Compost acts like a slow-release fertilizer.

Many gardeners feed plants with a blast of chemical fertilization that rapidly leaches through the soil and beyond the root zone, upsetting the soil web in the process. Compost instead provides a slow, gentle flow of nutrition to your plants.

15. Compost feeds the worms in your soil.

Worms tunnel through the ground opening up passages while leaving their nutrient-dense castings behind. They are nature's gentle little tilling machines, and they love to chow down on compost, dragging it down into the root zone.

16. Composting keeps organic matter out of the water supply.

Letting nitrogen-rich organic matter lie around increases the risk of contaminating water supplies. This can be seen on a large scale with factory farming, where massive concentrations of manure end up running off into local streams, ponds, lakes, and other bodies of water, causing unhealthy algae blooms and the proliferation of disease-causing bacteria. Composting allows for the healthy breakdown of "waste" materials before they end up in the wrong place.

17. Compost feeds the fungi in your soil.

Mushrooms and other fungi digest rocks, wood, and other debris, making minerals available to plants and trees. Compost gives them something (figuratively) to chew on.

18. Compost improves clay.

There's nothing like some good organic matter to moderate a heavy clay soil. Cracked, rocky, hard clay can be turned into loamy soil with repeated additions of compost.

19. Compost improves sand.

Sand is loose and lets water and nutrients run through. Compost helps it hold on to the good stuff for a lot longer.

20. Composting gives you gardening "street credibility."

Seriously, man. You don't compost? What kind of gardener are you?

21. Compost can fight erosion.

Adding organic matter to the soil allows it to both absorb more water and support more plant life. This gives compost-rich soils an advantage over neighboring ground in times of heavy rainfall.

22. Compost increases the nutrients in your vegetables.

When you feed the soil around your plants, you're feeding yourself. Healthy plants—and people—need a wide variety of micro nutrients. Good compost has them.

23. Composting keeps fertility on your property.

When you throw away your leaves, food scraps, and other organic matter, you are throwing away minerals you should be keeping on your homestead. Don't do it.

24. Composting regains some of the money you lose on food.

Did your toddler mangle his plate of peas and chicken and then walk away? Composting that failed meal means you regain a little of the energy you lost buying and preparing it.

25. Composting turns liabilities into assets.

When you have to pay to dispose of food scraps, poop, logs, and eggshells, they are liabilities. Turn them into compost, and they become assets.

26. Composting binds up toxins.

Studies have shown that some toxic substances can be rendered inert when they're composted and thereby incorporated into complex molecules. In an increasingly toxic world, it's good to know we can fight back a little.

27. Composting lets you be a little like God.

God created composting by engineering a massive nutrient-cycling machine: the earth. When you compost, you're following in His footsteps. When you throw stuff in the trash, you're totally being like the devil and we'll totally judge you for it.

28. Composting is recycling.

If you like recycling but don't compost, what's wrong with you? Even if you live in an apartment, you can compost. Save up your compostable goods and dump them by a tree in the woods once a week rather than throwing them in the trash.

29. Compost destroys pathogens and fights plant disease.

Compost is like yogurt. It's full of active cultures that will fight disease in your plants and in the soil. By feeding the soil web with compost, you increase its biological complexity and decrease the chances of a serious problem.

30. Compost loosens soil.

Roots need space in the soil and some air to breathe. Compost loosens and opens the ground, letting in some much-needed air.

31. Compost replaces fertilizer.

This is one less thing you need to buy!

32. And one last reason: compost is easy to make!

In this book I'm going to show you how to make compost in a variety of ways you've likely never imagined. You don't need thermometers, pitchforks, tumblers, or anything else to improve your soil.

Making compost can be easy and fun. Let's do it.

2. Say Goodbye to Boring Composting

Most of us have read articles on "how to compost." Some of us (like me… your friendly neighborhood mad scientist) have read many thousands of pages on the subject.

You've probably seen lists of what you can and cannot put into compost piles. We're going to question most of those things; but first, let's just start with the easy, standard composting rules.

To make compost, mix one part "green" material with one part "brown" material. Green materials are nitrogen-rich waste, such as manure or kitchen scraps. Brown materials are things like shredded paper, leaves, or wood chips. Experts recommend that you get a carbon to nitrogen ratio of 25–30 parts carbon to one part nitrogen. Since organic matter is mostly a combination of carbon and nitrogen, the "brown" and "green" one-to-one ratio is a simple way to remember it: when you mix in some sloppy waste from the kitchen, throw in some dry, brown waste from the yard. It's pretty easy.

If you compost in a bin, make sure the bin can contain at least a cubic yard of material. If you compost in a pile, aim for that same size at the very least. If you do it that large, you will get a nice hot pile provided materials are mixed appropriately and are wet enough to get going. If you go smaller than that, you'll still make compost, but it will take a lot longer. You also need to make sure the pile is thoroughly watered, then covered to retain heat and moisture.

If you listen to most experts, the process sounds like a pain in the neck! All the rules… all the stifling rules:

No meat!

No bread!

No oils!

No paper!

No sawdust!

No macaroni and cheese!

Make a nice set of boxes!

Make your boxes from cedar or block!

Don't make your boxes from evil toxic things!

Put hardware cloth around your bin!

Put in motion detectors for the rats!

Watch out for disease-carrying flies!

Get the C/N ratio right!

Ensure a thermophilic reaction!

Crush eggshells before adding them!

Ask your neighbors first!

Check with local authorities!

Are you sure you checked with local authorities?

Check with local authorities again!

Keep it moist but not wet!

Turn it monthly… weekly… daily… hourly!

Don't let it go anaerobic!

You need a barrel!

You need an aerating crank!

You need PVC aerating tubes!

You need a thermometer!

You need a worm bin!

You need an odor-free countertop compost container!

Making compost is serious business for some folks. Go on YouTube some day and start watching videos. You'll see homemade motorized compost sieves… scientists with huge thermometers… tractors turning steaming piles of carefully mixed debris…

It reminds me of the fitness-obsessed:

"Man, dude… I can bench 560…"

"Oh yeah? I can keep my compost cooking at 140 degrees for weeks."

"Whoa, man. Whoa. Now *that's* heavy!"

It's time to take a deep breath and rethink composting.

At a basic level, composting is just letting things rot. It's a simple process of nutrient recycling you can harness to feed your plants.

For years I was a typical composter. I made big piles of organic matter and did my best to layer greens and browns. I dragged home trash cans full of coffee grounds from a local espresso joint and layered them with leaves and rotten straw to get a good hot pile going. I'd mix in all of our kitchen scraps (with the exception of the "bad" stuff, such as meat, oils, etc.) and add all the grass clippings I could bag. Spent non-woody plants from the garden got thrown in, as did eggshells, hair, and shredded paper from the office.

I'd carefully water and turn the piles every week or two, getting excited when they heated up and wondering where I'd gone wrong when they failed to heat up.

As for where I put them... well, at the back of the yard, of course! Far from sight and smell! I built enclosures of various levels of aesthetic quality, from stacked landscape logs at one point to a nice pile of cinder blocks at another. I pressed large rings of hardware cloth into service, and sometimes I just made a pad of square pavers and piled organic matter on top of that.

My wife and I moved multiple times but we always had some sort of compost pile even when we were renting. It just felt like the right thing to do—and our children have been raised in the habit. When we visit a friend's house for dinner, the children invariably ask "where's the compost?" as they clear the plates from the table, then look confused when the homeowner tells them to just "throw the scraps away."

I was obsessed with getting it right, just like the muscleheads at the gym. Yet no matter how much organic matter I scrounged together, we never seemed to have enough compost.

Can you imagine *ever* having "enough" compost?

If you're making your own piles only from the agricultural-extension-approved "waste" that comes through your yard and kitchen, chances are you'll never have enough.

You need more biomass right at the beginning.

Once I realized this fact, I started asking questions. Scary questions. The kind of questions that get you shunned by your local garden club.

Questions such as:

> *Can you compost meat?*
>
> *Can you compost dog droppings?*
>
> *Can you use the fish guts from the local market?*
>
> *Can you use urine as a fertilizer?*
>
> *Can you use all the wood shavings from your carpenter neighbor?*
>
> *Can you compost Hot Pockets?*
>
> *Can you compost logs?*
>
> *Can you compost bones?*
>
> *Can you compost the contents of a bucket toilet without dying?*
>
> *Can you compost without all the work?*

Can you really make "enough" compost?

The answer to all those questions is yes!

If Nature does it, you can do it.

The reason extension agents don't recommend adding certain ingredients to your pile is because they can attract vermin, create odors, and fail to break down quickly in a typical backyard pile.

It's not because they're useless as soil amendments.

Look, human waste is a great fertilizer. Just observe the green grass over the top of a septic tank.

And wait... didn't the Indians have the Pilgrims bury fish carcasses under their corn?

And shucks... have you ever seen the rich crumbly soil beneath big fallen logs in a forest?

To get started right now, you don't really need bins or a mix of "browns and greens." Compost is like magic. Take "waste," and make it into a resource. Every bit of organic material found can be returned to the soil.

Every time I drive through town, I see piles of leaves, branches, grass clippings, tree trunks, pine needles, and other rich organic matter lying by the road, waiting to be picked up by waste management.

Why?

Because people don't realize what they're doing! By sending all that organic material off their property they're exporting their soil's fertility only to later purchase some back in plastic bags marked with numbers such as "10-10-10."

Think about it: a plant or a tree pulls up nutrients from deep in the soil and uses them, along with solar energy and water, to grow. All parts of that plant contain good things that can be used by your garden. Don't chuck all that tree's hard work by the side of the road to be taken to the dump. You'd be leaving your piece of earth less fertile than it was before.

Instead, compost! In the following pages I'll share a variety of composting methods from the simple to the very slightly less simple. This isn't a textbook for scientists or a resource for folks who like lots of numbers and figures. It's a book on thinking differently about feeding your soil. It's a guide to squeezing every bit of goodness out of the organic resources that come your way while growing the happiest plants you've ever grown.

It's time to get excited about composting again. It's time to quit worrying about ratios and "don'ts."

It's time to roll up your sleeves and learn to compost *everything*!

Let's get started by looking at the easiest way to make compost.

3. Composting for Anarchists

On a fine and sunny Sunday in the middle of a hot Florida summer, my family and I visited some friends for lunch after church. Our kids played together, we jammed on the piano and guitar, had a few glasses of wine, and talked theology and gardening. It was great. They're our kind of folks.

At one point, I noticed all the debris left over from lunch: watermelon rinds, half-finished plates of food, limp salad, etc., and I asked if they had a compost pile. The husband answered, "Yeah, we have one of those tumbler types, but I'm ashamed to say we don't really use it much." We walked out to the backyard, and he showed me a well-built, hand-cranked plastic composter.

"It just doesn't work all that well. I'm not sure how people get perfect compost from these things."

You know, I'm not sure either. I've had folks tell me about their wonderful tumblers, but my experience is less than exciting.

I understand the desire to solve the hassle of composting through science and design. A traditional pile with its accompanying need for turning requires work. I've tried finding easier ways myself, so I don't blame people for buying composting gadgets.

Heck, a few years ago I built a 55-gallon compost tumbler for my wife because she wanted an easier way to make compost for her square-foot gardens.

It was a marvel of ingenuity! A leap forward for upcycling! A high-capacity composter for cheapskates!

The problem was... it really wasn't all that easy to turn. It was also not big enough to cook down properly, meaning that the kitchen scraps sat in there in a big clump without breaking down.

This is a common problem even with the nice compost tumblers you buy from nice stores or out of the back of nice gardening magazines. It's not just a problem that arises in redneck drum composters.

Another problem you'll often face when using a tumbler is incomplete compost creation. That is, unless you have two of them, at some point you need to quit dumping in your food scraps for a month or so in order to let the compost break down completely. You also need to mist the contents with a hose and crank it regularly.

How many of you are willing to do all that for a couple of buckets of compost?

As a final indignity, decent compost tumblers are expensive.

The real silliness in this fight to make perfect compost through science is that Nature recycles organic matter into compost all the time without tumblers, cranks, bins, sifters, pitchforks, garden hoses, or thermometers.

Do you know how Nature makes compost?

She throws things on the ground.

That's most of it right there. Throwing things on the ground.

Easy, right? Just throw things on the ground.

Let me paint a picture for you.

Imagine a bear shuffling through the woods on a warm fall afternoon. Suddenly his nose twitches, and he looks up.

Mmm, he thinks… *there's something sweet up ahead… smells like…*

Honey!

Growing more excited as the sweet smell fills his nostrils, the bear finally finds the source of the delicious aroma. At the edge of a sunny clearing stands a long-dead tree… and there, in its hollow trunk, thousands of worker bees have carefully gathered together the essences of a million flowers to feed their young through the winter and continue the noble race of *apis mellifera.*

The bear doesn't care about their hard work. He wants lunch.

The bear starts rocking the dead tree back and forth, back and forth as the bees fly into a fury. The victims fight back as best as they can, but the bear is not deterred. There's a sudden *crack*! The tree falls, bursts apart, and spills bees, larvae, honey, and comb across the ground.

As the bees circle in terrified panic, the bear chews his way through the delicious comb, eating larvae, pollen, honey, and wax together, glutting himself on the hard-won ambrosia of the now-shattered bee colony.

Finally satiated, the bear leaves… but not before leaving some bear-sized droppings behind.

Over the next few days the remaining survivors of the bear attack clean up what's left of the honey and buzz off with their queen in search of a new home… and the remains of the battle are covered by drifts of autumn leaves. A year later there's no comb to be found… no bear droppings… and what's left of the fallen tree is starting to crumble as mushrooms erupt from the rotten wood.

Five years later the log is gone as well. In its place, a few fine young oak saplings are reaching toward the sun above, taking advantage of the fertile soil and the gap in the tree canopy.

And the bear? He later repented of his bee-destroying ways and became a noted spokesbear for a famous Bee Rights organization.

Just kidding. Bees, sadly, don't have rights.

When organic matter falls to the ground, it enriches the soil and fosters the growth of new plants. Dead material is reused by living material, which eventually dies and is then recycled into living material again.

It happens over and over again in a vast array of patterns. Worms consume leaves and are then eaten by birds. The birds spatter their droppings across the forest floor, feeding the trees. The trees then grow more leaves which eventually fall to the ground and feed the worms… and the cycle continues.

Using this cycle to your benefit is truly as simple as throwing things on the ground.

You don't need a nice pile. You don't need hardware cloth. You don't need a pitchfork.

You just need organic matter. If it's in contact with the soil, it will break down.

The soil is an amazing digester of organic materials. It's a place filled with bacteria and fungi, worms and beetles, ants and termites, earwigs and millipedes. All of these little deconstruction machines will deal with whatever falls to the ground and transform it into rich humus for your plants and trees.

If you're not concerned with collecting sifted, finished compost you can dole it out by the teaspoonful to your pepper plants and you are composting without work. Throw it on the ground!

Of course, why would you need to collect the finished compost? Nature doesn't. She just lets organic matter collect and decompose where it falls.

Want to make compost like Nature does? Throw stuff on the ground.

If you eat a banana in the car, you can throw the peel out the window by the side of the road and it will provide nutrition to whatever lucky plants happen to be at the end of its flight path. Likewise, if you're smoking a cigar and stub out the butt on the ground, if it's made of organic material it will feed something.

If you're interested in composting with the least amount of work in the most natural way possible, here's how you do it.

Step 1: Find Some Organic Matter

An avocado skin? Great. Moldy baked beans? Wonderful. Old bills and non-glossy junk mail? Sure. Eggshells, tea bags, cardboard, citrus peels? Yep.

It makes sense to keep a small trash can with a tight lid in your kitchen. Anything compostable goes in there. Even an old coffee can works well.

When you're pruning fruit trees or dealing with fallen oak limbs in the yard, don't drag them to the side of the road for disposal or burn them in a pile.

If you have a picnic in the yard with the children, use uncoated paper plates. Then save them... along with whatever uneaten food the children leave behind.

If you feel like working a little harder to gather organic matter, you'll find opportunities everywhere.

When you have a potluck dinner at church, help clean up at the end, and throw all the napkins and food scraps into one container you can then take home.

Check with your local coffee shop and see if you can pick up grounds from them.

See if you can get boxes of expired produce from your local grocery store or farm stand.

Gather cardboard from alleyways.

Ask your local feed store if you can sweep up the straw and alfalfa that falls to the ground from their bales. I've gathered a LOT of material this way.

Ask your neighbors to dump their yard waste at your place.

Collect shredded documents from work.

Pick up bags of leaves by the side of the road in fall.

Ask local tree companies if they'll drop their fresh-chipped "waste" in your yard.

If you want maximum fertility on your little piece of the earth, collect everything organic you can find all the time.

And then, my anarchist friend, move on to step 2.

Step 2: Throw It On the Ground

Once a week or more, take your kitchen-scrap trashcan to a place that needs fertility, then dump it. Do the same with your yard waste: drag it to wherever the soil looks a bit sad and throw it on the ground.

What does this look like in practice?

Well, fruit trees need fertilizing, right? Normally you'd give them a hit of chemical fertilizer now and again throughout the year. Instead of doing that, just drop organic matter on the ground around them. Pretend the tree's root zone is a big, rough, compost pile. Chop up some sticks, throw down some paper plates, spatter rotten salad greens, and throw in some spoiled fruit. It's easy and fun. You can also put hunks of logs near the bases of your trees and along the edge of pathways and gardens to act as bunkers for fungi and other beneficial organisms.

Don't worry about making everything neat and tidy—nature doesn't! If it really bothers you to have things looking a bit rough for a while, keep a little pile of mulch on hand. When you dump coffee filters or office papers and other ugly debris, cover it with mulch so it can decompose without offending your eyes (or the eyes of the fascists at Code Enforcement).

Here's something to consider, however: if you make a big pile of sticks it might take a long, long time to break down. That's because there's too much air circulating around the wood that keeps it too dry for quick decay. Contact with the ground makes all the difference. If you have sticks, bust them up a bit. Smaller pieces mean there is more surface area for decay organisms to chew on.

If you've got a large area you'd like to improve, don't scatter your organic matter too thinly. It's better to highly improve a small area than it is to very slightly increase the fertility of a large area. Do it section by section. Why's that? Because you'll get better yields. If you have twenty trees that are struggling and you give each of them a pint of compost, you'll still have twenty trees that are struggling and you're not likely to get much fruit next year. However, if you took twenty pints of compost and gave it to one or two trees... well, those trees are going to be happy for a change and are much more likely to bear something tasty in the spring.

Direct Composting in the Garden

When it comes to annual gardening you can also use the power of "throw it on the ground" to improve patches that fail to produce well.

In my vegetable gardens I pick one of my 4' x 12' beds and designate it as the compost pile for a year. On that bed go all the spent vegetable plants from the other garden plots, along with the weeds, kitchen scraps, rotten pumpkins, etc. A lot of fertility is gained by that space over the 365 days that the pile lies there and rots. At the end of the year, I might shovel the uncomposted waste in the bed over to the bed next door and garden where the pile had been... or I might just smash it down a bit, mulch on top, then plant vegetable transplants right into the heap.

As a bonus, during the course of the year, your compost pile bed will often bear a yield.

For some reason, squash, melons, and tomatoes all love volunteering in compost piles. If any seeds have gone into your kitchen bucket and out the door into your compost pile/garden bed, chances are they're going to pop up at some point. One year we got cantaloupes from our garden bed/compost pile. Another year we got loofah gourds. And tomatoes? Oh yes.

There's another benefit to throwing your scraps right onto a garden bed: it's less work that putting all your scraps in a designated composting area, then later taking the final product and wheeling it over to your garden beds. When you drop organic matter into an unused bed, it's right where it needs to be.

Furthermore, have you ever seen how nice and green the weeds get around the edges of a compost pile? That's because some of the fertility in the pile is running off into the ground around your stack of compost. When you compost directly in a gardening area, you let the good material go straight down into the soil where you'll later be growing vegetables for your table.

It just makes sense.

Last year we buried some buckets of fresh manure in a lousy garden bed, then chucked all our kitchen scraps on top. At one point the mound of decaying compost was over two feet tall. Because of the size of the bed, that two foot depth represented a lot of organic material.

Compost piles in Florida end up infested with fire ants, and that's exactly what happened to this one. I basically had to run up to it and throw my compost before the swarming ants injected me with venom and stripped the flesh from my bones. The only way to eliminate these pests is to poison them, and I wasn't about to poison my compost pile so I let them be. I'm sure the turning, chewing, tunneling, and excreting done by the ants increases the breakdown of the pile. I guess you could call that a silver lining, though there's really not much to like about stinging ants.

Enough about fire ants. I'm already feeling ghost stings on my ankles just thinking about them.

We stacked our pile high and threw kitchen scraps on it every evening. Some of these remains included some Seminole pumpkin guts, which led to something amazing the next year.

In the spring I noticed a wide variety of plants popping up here and there on the pile. There were some ugly potato plants, some sprawling tomatoes, a decent amount of weeds (mostly Spanish needle, also known in Latin as *Bidens*), mango and avocado seedlings, and some sort of vigorous melon-like vine. When I first saw the vines I assumed they were cantaloupes, but after a couple of months they started setting fruit, and it rapidly became apparent that they weren't melons; they were pumpkins!

They didn't stop inside the compost pile/garden bed, however.

The ridiculously supercharged pumpkin vines sprawled over hundreds of square feet of space, climbing up into the lower branches of one of my peach trees, running over one of my water chestnut ponds, jumping the path into my sugar cane beds, attempting to smother my son's yacon bed, and completely covering several adjacent beds, rendering them unplantable. Wherever the vines grew, they added more roots to their stems, but the healthiest portions of the plants were near the original compost pile.

The pumpkin vines certainly made a mess of my garden, but I left them alone regardless. That mess was a ridiculously productive mess! We blew through one hundred pounds of delicious, buttery Seminole pumpkins (their fine flesh tastes like a cross between a great butternut squash and an excellent sweet potato) before the end of July. For a few weeks in the heat of August they quit producing, then jumped right back into production as the days cooled off in September. From spring until frost they rocked that compost pile garden bed. The final tally reached almost two hundred pounds of pumpkins.

Now here's the funny thing: I planted this same variety of pumpkin in my front yard food forest and had only minimal luck. In fact, the seeds that grew in the compost were from the few fruit we'd harvested off those disappointing vines the previous year. Yet the plants in the front yard were blah, and the vines pouring from the compost pile were triumphantly abundant.

There's something we can learn here.

Just think about how well some plants do growing directly on a compost pile. The three that really seem to thrive in my compost piles are tomatoes, squash, and melons.

Even if you turn your compost pile, some of the seeds always survive the heat and start growing when you spread compost elsewhere—or they grow directly on the pile like my Seminole pumpkins. This is why you shouldn't indiscriminately throw weed debris in your compost pile and assume the seeds will get cooked. Well-meaning composting instructors aside, seeds always seem to come through.

Now why would tomatoes, squash, etc. do so well in a still-warm pile of rotting organic material? In nature, fruits fall to the ground and rot. At some point in the future, provided they aren't eaten by scavengers, the seeds usually sprout in a big mess. They are then thinned by cutworms, the weather, and competition. Eventually a few of the hundreds or thousands of seeds (fertility of the soil and weather conditions permitting) will manage to grow into adulthood and reproduce.

Your compost pile is like a huge concentrated stack of nutrition. It's no wonder some plants thrive in that situation.

So consider this experiment: what if a gardener deliberately constructed compost piles as garden plots for those species that love to grow in compost? What if he simply piled up a mess of hot organic matter in the fall and threw tomatoes, melons, and squash on top of it to weather out the winter and erupt into life in the spring?

Nature does it, and that makes it worth a try.

Direct Composting in a Banana Circle

Permaculture enthusiasts in tropical to subtropical climates love making a specialized type of garden/compost pile called a "banana circle."

The basic concept is simple: bananas crave water and are vora-
cious feeders that love lots of organic matter.

In order to hold on to water and nutrition, make a roughly yard-
deep circular indentation in the ground. Angle it to trap runoff,
leaving one end open to the flow of water across your property, or
run a drainpipe off your roof, set up an outdoor shower or urinal,
or do what I did: run the water from the kitchen sink out of the
house.

Around the edges of that pit, mound up the dirt taken from
the center. You will be planting your bananas in the edge mound
along with other plants that will benefit from the soon-to-be moist
conditions and high fertility of the circle.

Where does the fertility come from? That's the fun part! In
the middle of your newly dug circle, start dumping a lot of organic
matter. Chunks of log, straw, manure, kitchen scraps, chopped
weeds, Spanish moss, fish guts, coffee grounds, sugarcane waste,
feathers, newspapers, and whatever else you can find. Make a nice
big mound; it will rot down quickly.

After you've done that, mulch well over the bare soil, and start
planting on the berm around the pile in the center. Bananas are the
keystone of this design, so plant them first, and then start adding
plants in between. Toward the center, where the soil will be more
damp, add moisture-loving plants such as cannas, malanga, or taro.
At the top of the berm, consider planting lemongrass, comfrey, sage,
yacon, and other species that don't mind it drier. On the outside of
the berm, try planting cassava, chaya, squash, and other edibles. A
ground cover of sweet potatoes is often recommended, as that adds
one more layer of edibility to the design, and the rapidly growing

vines keep weeds under control.

As you plant, make sure to leave a gap in the edge of the circle so you can continue to throw organic matter on the compost heap in the center.

This system will digest a remarkable amount of organic matter while paying you back in food. If you live farther north, you'll obviously have to forgo the bananas and other tropical plant species, yet the basic design will still work. You'll just have to do some experimentation… but isn't that half the fun of gardening?

Building a banana circle beats having to turn multiple piles or buy a tumbler, then sift and haul the resulting compost to your plants. By dropping the items to compost in the middle of a gardening area, you save a lot of work.

And of course, if the couple of hours it takes to build a banana circle is still too much work for you, just throw stuff on the ground! It will rot, and as it does so, the fertility of your ground will improve along with your harvests.

4. Making Your Bed With Sheet Composting

Okay, so maybe "throwing it on the ground" is a little too anarchistic for you.

I understand. Nature is a wild and terrifying place. We don't necessarily want our yards to look crazy. Plus, in nature you don't often come across anything as ugly as junk mail. It's true: just throwing things on the ground doesn't always look nice, though everything does eventually break down.

Enter sheet composting, also known as sheet mulching, lasagna gardening, deep mulch gardening, "Back to Eden" gardening, etc.

Basically, the idea here is that you put down some kind of weed-crushing compostable material like cardboard or newspaper, then pile organic matter on top of that and follow it with a thick layer of mulch.

The original deep mulching queen is undoubtedly Ruth Stout. I have a lot of respect for Mrs. Stout. She was quite a person, as a glance through one of her books will rapidly reveal. Her book *Gardening Without Work: for the Aging, the Busy & the Indolent*[1] has been a cult classic since the 1950s, and the method has come into new popularity recently thanks to author Patricia Lanza and her book *Lasagna Gardening: A New Layering System for Bountiful Gardens: No Digging, No Tilling, No Weeding, No Kidding!*[2] The inspiring recent film *Back to Eden* also features a variant of this method as used by farmer Paul Gautschi.[3]

Proponents of deep mulching brag that this method requires no tilling, no weeding, and almost no work. For the most part, they're right… that is, *after* the system is installed. On the front end, this takes some serious work.

The deep mulch garden uses layers of mulch to crush weeds, keep the soil moist, and add organic matter. If you're gardening on clay, it also has a major loosening effect over time. Stout's preferred mulch was straw—rotten or fresh, but she advocated using whatever organic matter you could scavenge. If you go for the modern "Lasagna gardening" incarnation, you put down a layer of cardboard or newspapers right over a patch of weeds or lawn, then stack a foot or two of varied organic materials on top of that, including compost, manure, straw, leaves, or whatever you have available. Plant into that and… instant garden! As weeds pop up—if they pop up, smother them with straw.

Bam! Dead!

The great thing about sheet composting is what it does for your soil. As an example, I had a few red oak trees removed from my yard several years ago. When the men from the tree company took them down, they chopped up the trunks and larger branches and started raking great big piles of smaller sticks and leaves together. That gave me an idea. Why not pile those in a corner of my yard and let them compost? The tree crew happily obliged, and we stacked them up.

The next spring, the debris had settled. Curious to see what the ground was like beneath, I started digging. What had formerly been dead grey sand was now a rich, black loam, filled with earthworms and soil life. That dirt is now some of the best in my yard. No tilling, no fertilizing or adding of amendments. Just a big stack of organic matter left to rot in place, and I was looking at grade A soil.

Imagine doing the same in your garden plot. I've done it multiple times now, and I can assure you that the results are impressive. If you've got bad soil, sandy soil, or even clay, a deep layer of mulch will fix it.

Another benefit of this method is that it's easier than traditional composting. Just chuck your leaves, kitchen scraps, cardboard, etc. into the garden and bury them as needed. The soil life that results is impressive.

When I lived in Tennessee, sheet mulching transformed a patch of hard clay and Bermuda grass into a rich patch of loamy gardening paradise. Over time, the clay darkened and loosened beneath my beds. I was amazed by the transformation. Tilling had been a nightmare, but sheet mulching finally gave me something amazing to work with.

One final benefit of this method is water conservation. Over time, the ground became so rich with humus that it acted as a sponge. Even during long dry spells, the layers beneath the surface were cool and moist. You can see in this in the *Back to Eden* film as well: the side-by-side comparison of rich garden soil and the dry baked dirt elsewhere on Gautschi's property is astounding.

Now here's the downside: if you're going to sheet mulch over any kind of area, you'd better get used to dragging stuff home and piling it up. Sheet mulching isn't really an easy alternative to other forms of gardening, despite Ruth Stout's assurances that it's "no work."

Why?

Because you spend all your time scrounging for materials.

Sheet mulching isn't something you can do half-way, like chucking kitchen scraps around the base of a tree. Getting lots of wood chips, straw, stable bedding, leaves, pine needles, straw, compost and other mulching materials isn't easy. If you don't own a truck and don't have friends with large farms or livestock, finding and transporting enough material to deeply cover even a small area is a pain. You don't want to just put down an inch or two of mulch; you want to put down a foot. When you do that, the weeds don't have a chance. If you skimp, you'll pay for it.

Ever try hoeing in mulch? It's a royal pain.

Another downside: back in Ruth Stout's day, straw and manure weren't contaminated with long-term herbicides like the infinitely evil Grazon from Dow AgroSciences (more on that later in this book). When you sheet compost today, you're often relying on materials from outside your homestead—materials that may end up killing your garden for the next five years. That's a risk I'm not willing to take. I don't trust hay, straw, or manure anymore. I got nailed once, and that was enough.

Additionally, I listed one of the benefits of sheet mulching as its ability to foster worms and other soil life. Unfortunately, this also carries over to slugs and snails. The second year I had a mulch garden, I ended up with an incredible amount of slugs. After a week of trapping and killing them, I was free; yet they never would have been a problem without all the nice, moist mulch they'd been breeding in.

Sheet composting simply makes no sense if you're going to garden on any kind of decent acreage. The materials are simply too tough to acquire in quantity or to deal with. If you had a modest one-eighth acre garden, covering it with mulch would almost be a full-time job. This may be a good method for small spaces, but it's not good for larger plots.

That doesn't mean you should avoid this method. It's a great tool for smaller spaces. If you're setting up a small garden and have a good bit of organic matter to compost, this is a wonderful way to improve soil.

Let's take a look at how to do it.

How to Sheet Mulch

First, pick your garden plot, and mark out the edges. If it's full of tall grass or weeds, mow it down, leave the clippings in place, and water thoroughly. You want it wet before you cover the ground with mulch, otherwise you'll be trapping in dryness, not moisture.

Next, get yourself a bunch of cardboard or newspaper and cover the entire space, overlapping to make sure nothing comes through. The same applies to newspaper: a nice thick layer is best. Though some will say you can get away with a single layer of cardboard or roughly six sheets of newspaper, two or three times that is better. When I was dealing with (I should say pulling my hair out and screaming at) Bermuda grass, it took multiple layers of cardboard over the nasty stuff before I could beat it. Any gap and the rhizomes would find their way through and re-infest my garden.

After your initial weed-block layer is down, wet that as well. This will help it stay in place so you can start adding mulch. (What kind of mulch is best? We'll talk about that at the end of this chapter.) A good mix is what you should shoot for. Basically, you're composting in place, so if you can mix grass clippings with pine bark, straw with manure, leaves with coffee grounds, etc., things will break down better. A wider range of plant material also means a wider range of nutrients for your garden space. The main thing to remember is: stack it high with whatever you can get and keep watering as you go. Get this mess at least a foot deep.

If you want to plant right away, you can pull back some of the mulch, add pockets of compost, then plant seeds or transplants. The best results, however, come a year or so after you've established your garden patch. By that point, the cardboard has rotted away and you've hopefully added mulch on top a few more times as the previous layers have settled. The ground beneath is now full of life and compost, and your plants are strong and healthy from the abundance of moisture in the soil. See some weeds that managed to peek through? Throw yesterday's bad news on them or suffocate them with mulch. Once you've done the groundwork, the deep mulch garden is pretty easy to maintain. Never till it under, or you'll undo all your hard work.

There's plenty to love about the deep mulch/Back to Eden/Ruth Stout/Lasagna gardening method of piling on organic matter. There's also plenty to loathe. After multiple years of fiddling with the various incarnations of "stack and forget" gardening, I still occasionally use it when I have the materials, but as my plots have expanded, I find less and less reason to pile tons of organic matter into my annual gardens.

I am, however, a big fan of using mulch to fix the soil—particularly around fruit trees and shrubs, even if I don't build my vegetable gardens with massive amounts of it.

So, What's the Best Mulch?

Sometimes you get blessed with large amounts of mulching material, such as when a neighbor "forgets" where her property line lies and starts dumping the contents of her horse stalls at the edge of your woods, or when you manage to catch a local tree company clearing trees and vines along the power lines and shredding them into delicious chips.

One of the greatest benefits of mulch is its ability to feed the soil as it decomposes, making life better for the soil web and fungi in particular, which in turn makes your plants happier. Another benefit is the ability of mulch to hold in moisture yet still be permeable to the air. Plastic doesn't allow that. Rock mulches are better than manufactured products like plastic, tire rubber shreds, etc., but they still don't give you the benefit of adding organic matter to the soil.

Here's my gut response on inorganic mulches: they're only useful in very specific applications. If you're interested in killing off a big area of grass, laying down black plastic or tarps works well. Long-term, though, you end up with sun-baked crackly bits of plastic everywhere, trashing your yard.

As for rocks, if you've ever had young children, you know that a patch of gravel manages to get redistributed here and there across your yard over time—and I have the pebble-filled sippy cup to prove it.

I will admit that if you're going to set up a small nursery area or keep down weeds in a commercial-style row of grapes or blackberries, professional-grade woven weed block plastic is nice to have. But in the garden or food forest? Naw. We need mulch to fill more functions than that. And this being a book on composting, well…

organic matter is where it's at.

Just about any organic matter is better than nothing. Leaves, straw, and pine needles are good, but some are better than others in certain instances.

As a quick example, pine mulches—either needles or bark—are good for blueberries. Blueberries enjoy the acidity. In my opinion, it's not great for vegetable gardens. There I prefer to use leaves, straw, or rough-ground mulch from a tree company.

Cedar mulch, though quite popular, breaks down too slowly to help with soil improvement, plus it repels some beneficial organisms. I'd avoid it unless it's the only thing you can get, or if you're working on a landscape job where the mulch needs to stay looking good long-term. A better option is pine nuggets since they break down a little faster and look good for a long time.

Leaves make a good mulch, though some species tend to mat up and make it hard for the soil to breathe. Better to mix them in with other mulch, compost, straw, etc.

And speaking of straw, make sure you know where it comes from if you buy it. Remember: straw is sometimes contaminated with herbicides and pesticides that can cause long-term harm.

And that stable bedding I mentioned earlier? Generally good, though I'd let it rot for quite a while before I use in a vegetable garden. I'd also top it off with another kind of mulch, since horse manure in particular is often a big weed seed vector.

My favorite mulch is just the aforementioned stuff from tree companies (like Paul Gautschi uses). I've seen crews clearing the power line easements in my neighborhood and had them drop mulch in my yard. They're often glad to do so, since it saves them the cost of dumping it. Similarly, there are often city programs where all the "yard waste" gets tub ground into rough mulch.

The problem here, though, is that you don't know what went into the original mix. When I see the tree companies clearing the edges of my street, I can see what's going into the mix. The neighborhood contains oaks, hickory, wild grapes, palms, sumacs, etc. All healthy wild trees. Unfortunately, when you get mulch from a municipality, you could be bringing in diseases, herbicides, pesticides, etc. What if someone threw in a pear tree that was infected with fireblight? Or a row of dead blackberries, infected with a virus? You could bring those problems to your garden, orchard, or food forest. It's maybe worth the risk... or maybe not.

Keep your eyes open for tree companies doing line-clearing work, or make a few phone calls. Though it tends to rob nitrogen when fresh, a great big pile of half-rotten mulch comprised of the leaves and trunks of a variety of wild species makes a great addition to your gardening projects.

Enough About Mulch. What Else Can I Sheet Compost?

I used to have a lousy section of soil in my front yard food forest. Nothing was really happy out there... until one year when I hit pay dirt. Thanks to a woman with a non-profit animal rescue, I was hooked up with a constant stream of expired produce from a local grocery store. We're talking up to ten boxes a week of limp salad mixes, moldy berries, bruised fruit, putrid squashes, and green potatoes. Perfect!

Along with the mulch I was able to claim from a local tree company, I had enough organic material to sheet compost a decent chunk of my front yard food forest. Sometimes it just takes a little patience and looking around. Ask enough people and keep your eyes open, and the opportunities will eventually come your way.

Since I was interested in killing off some of the weeds and grass around my trees, I gathered together some cardboard and put it down as a weed-block layer as described above. I then threw lots and lots of expired produce on top of it.

After stacking up the produce layer, it was time to throw on some mulch from the friendly tree service guys.

That made it look more normal out there, rather than looking like someone threw grenades at a produce stand. Other things I added along with the mulch were some tree limbs, bamboo canes, and even chunks of tree trunk. Those are like fungal bunkers that will break down slowly over a few years while harboring insects and retaining moisture. Again, these tree trunk chunks were "trash" from another friend who was clearing out the yard of a rental house. Rather than going to the dump, he obligingly threw the chopped-up wood and other yard debris into a pile at the front of my food forest.

Yet another bit of "trash" I used came from another neighbor who had trimmed his oaks and was going to take the limbs to the dump. I told him to drop them at my place instead, so he did. I think he thought I was nuts, but I don't care. Those nice hardwood limbs were destined to become biochar (and yes, we will talk about biochar soon!). Before I mulched, I threw in lots of that biochar with the rotting produce. It would hold in nutrients and provide precious living space for a wide variety of microscopic life.

So, to review, I fixed a chunk of crummy soil with:

1. Free expired produce

2. Free shredded tree waste

3. Free chunks of wood from a rental house

4. Free tree branches turned into biochar

It's trash to treasure—literally!

You wouldn't believe the difference in tree and plant growth I've seen in my food forest since that year of rotten produce and tree company mulch. The peach and plum trees that sat sadly for years have suddenly filled out, the mulberry tree has blessed us with buckets of sweet fruit, and sweet potatoes, squashes, and flowers now twine over what used to be hard-baked sand and patchy brown grass. That's the wonder of composting. Sheet composting is a great way to claim a piece of ground without having to pull weeds or till. It's also a nice way to compost right in place and it greatly improves the soil long-term.

So, do you think sheet composting rotten vegetables and logs in your front yard is weird?

You haven't seen anything yet—it's time to bring out the worms!

5. Redneck Vermicomposting

It was a warm, sunny day as my six-year-old self played beside the canal in my grandpop's backyard in south Florida. Dad was doing some yard work there, and I was simply enjoying being a kid. Palm tree fronds swayed gently in the breeze, and the ripples in their immaculately kept swimming pool spattered sparkling lights across the ceiling of the back porch.

I remember watching the fish and blue crabs in the brown water along the sea wall and marveling at the strange little spiders hanging inside the screened-in pool enclosure. They looked just like green bird droppings.

At some point on that pretty afternoon, I found a little red earthworm and took it to Dad to show him. Always patient, he stopped raking under the coconut palms for a moment and said, "Oh, I see you found a little dinky worm!"

I thought Dinky Worm was a good name for my new pet. I remember talking to Dinky Worm and singing songs about Dinky Worm as I sat on the seawall.

And then I accidentally let Dinky Worm fall into the brackish water below. It happened so fast there was nothing I could do. One moment he was safe in my hand... and in the next moment I was watching his wriggling form vanish beneath the sluggish brown water.

"Dinky Worm!" I yelled. "Nooooooooo!!!"

It took a long time for Dad to comfort me.

In retrospect, I think I was a total pain in the neck as a child.

What does this have to do with anything? Everything! This tragic moment set the stage for my lifelong love of worms. Though I killed the first one I ever caught, I've raised many, many more since then and kept them in fine shape. (Granted, I no longer sit on seawalls while handling worms. That's a large part of my current success.)

Why would one want to raise worms? Because they're God's little compost-creation machines. Keeping a bin or a bed of them on your property is an easy way to create great compost while also honoring the Most Blessed Memory of Dinky Worm.

Now, if there's a way to make things complicated, someone will find it... then post a "how to" on the Internet. From composting to container gardening, there's always a difficult and time-consuming way to do a project that should be easy.

If you look up "composting with worms," you'll find detailed instructions on care, feeding, building worm bins, etc. There's a lot of good info out there—don't get me wrong, but there are also a lot of folks selling high-tech setups that are way beyond the basic systems needed to keep worms happy.

If you're on a budget and thought you couldn't get started in the world of worms, take heart. Let me show you just how easy keeping worms can be.

Why Compost With Worms?

First things first. Before we get into worm housing and care, we have to answer the question "why?" Why would you want to share your life with these creatures when there are easier ways to compost?

In the case of worms, it's quality, not quantity. The castings that emerge from the back end of worms are simply the highest quality compost in the world. There's no other compost that matches the fertility and the beneficial bacteria found in worm droppings.

Beyond those marvelous castings, you also get to harvest "worm tea," the fluid exudates you can collect from the bottom of your worm bin if you plan things out correctly. This stuff is like magic gardening elixir. If you want super happy and healthy plants, give them worm tea. Even if you never harvest any castings, worm composting is worth it for the worm tea.

What Kind of Worms?

Regular earthworms dig deep tunnels and aren't all that happy living containerized lives. The same goes for those big creepy night crawlers you find in puddles after a hard rain.

The main worm used for composting in worm bins is *Eisenia fetida*, also known as the red wiggler, the manure worm, or the tiger worm. Unlike soil-dwelling worms, these guys (I use the term loosely since they're hermaphroditic) like to live in piles of leaves, manure, and other decaying organic matter.

Another species sometimes used for vermicomposting is *Eudrilus eugeniae*, known colloquially as the African night crawler. (My friend Mart Hale[4] tried these guys out since they were touted as being significantly larger and more vigorous than red wigglers. Unfortunately, their vigor also extended to their desire to escape. At some point they decided to wiggle off, never to be seen again. He now recommends using a container that has an inward-facing rim they can't climb over.)

Though there are a variety of worms you can experiment with, I've stuck with the tried and true red wiggler. They're consistent composters, good breeders, and just generally hard to screw up. They also stay put.

Worms can be purchased online from a variety of sites. If you're lucky, you might even find someone locally that will share with you (thanks, Larry Grim![5]).

You don't need to buy a huge amount to get started, though it will kick-start your operation. My current worm bin is loaded with worms and it began with a handful that bred over time to become a majestic herd. I recommend jumping in by buying 500–1,000 worms. This will likely run you about $20.00.

Of course, before you buy your worms, you should have a place to keep them. Let's do that first, and let's do it as cheaply as possible.

Making a Redneck Worm Bin

My first couple of worm bins were pretty simple little things I built myself. All I did was buy two plastic storage bins and start doing surgery.

One bin became the bottom. Its job was to catch the "worm tea" that would drip from the drainage holes in the second bin. The second (top) bin had ¼-inch holes drilled all over the bottom of it for drainage, then it was nested into the first (bottom) bin on top of some 1½-inch pieces of wood that acted as spacers to keep the fluid levels from reaching its bottom.

The cover of the bottom bin was discarded. The cover of the top bin had large holes drilled in it with window screening glued over them so the worms would get enough air. That was the whole setup.

As for the initial fill for the worms, I used shredded paper and cardboard. All you need to do is get a bunch of waste paper (old bills, non-glossy junk mail, scrap paper from your printer, etc.) together, wet it thoroughly (a sink or bathtub works well), then squeeze out all the extra moisture and stuff it all in your new bin, making sure you get it at least two-thirds of the way full. After that, be sure to get a few handfuls of sand to sprinkle in there. Much like chickens, worms need some grit to help them digest.

Once that's done, add the worms. I usually feed them a little bit to start. Some carrot peels, an apple core or two, or perhaps a cantaloupe rind. Not too much, though. They need to get acclimated, plus the paper is good food for them.

Technically, this first worm bin was supposed to work indoors without smelling bad or breeding flies. Unfortunately, though it excluded house flies, little fruit flies were always finding it. It also didn't have a high enough capacity for our family. I discovered this when I threw in a rotten watermelon before going on vacation for a week. When I got back, the fluid from the watermelon had flooded the bin and most of the worms had either drowned or abandoned ship. Fortunately it was in the carport at the time and not in my kitchen.

After my initial experiments with small indoor bins like that one, I decided it was time to go big. This is where the redneck comes in.

One fine fall season we bought a new house in Tennessee. In

that house was a refrigerator that was on its last legs. After a few months, it completely gave up and forced us to buy a new one.

Seeing the dead fridge gave me a thought. What if I were to turn that nice, big, insulated metal and plastic container into a worm/compost bin? The capacity was incredible! Imagine all the castings I could make!

The first thing I did was remove the heavy door of the refrigerator so children couldn't get stuck in it. Then I stacked some cinder blocks in a forested back corner of the yard to act as supports for my ready made compost bin.

I dragged the fridge back there on a hand truck, then took out most of its guts. Then I tipped it onto its back, positioned it on top of the cinder blocks and threw a piece of plywood over the top as a cover.

Ta-da! Compost time!

Since the old refrigerator looked ugly as sin and was visible from the road, I spray painted it black and green which effectively rendered it invisible thanks to the surrounding bushes.

My next problem was getting a bunch of organic matter to fill it up and make the worms happy. I got bags of shredded paper from work, leaves from the neighbors, plus coffee grounds and kitchen scraps. Then I went dumpster diving a few times and brought home a bunch of rotten produce. I also added lots of leaves.

Once the refrigerator bin was suitably filled, I added some worms from my indoor plastic bin. I was nervous that my worms wouldn't survive the cold of winter outdoors so I made sure to keep some indoors just in case.

It turns out I didn't need to bother. That refrigerator, with its accompanying insulation and lots of decaying organic matter providing heat, kept my worms safely through the cold. It probably also helped that it was located in a sheltered woody area. That system worked wonderfully for years and provided my garden beds with a decent amount of incredibly rich compost.

Unfortunately, when I eventually moved from Tennessee back to my home state of Florida, I had to leave the fridge behind. Since I couldn't just abandon my workers (or their black gold), I gave away the compost and the worms to a few gardening friends before leaving.

Now I keep worms in a broken dishwasher placed on its back with some irrigation holes drilled for drainage. No special bins, no expensive worm food, no hassle.

You can definitely come up with some really slick ways to harvest lots more castings with less work, and some companies will sell you neat multi-tiered systems that take advantage of your worms' natural desire to move to where the food is—but you don't need that to get started. All you need is some redneck ingenuity.

Make Your Own Redneck Worm Bin

Here's how you can make a free worm bin in four easy steps:

Step 1: Find a Container

Worms aren't picky. If I can keep worms in plastic bins, old refrigerators, and broken dishwashers, you can find something that will work with a little scrounging.

Since red wigglers aren't really "diggers" like their cousins the earthworms, they just need a foot or two of moist organic matter to stay happy. That makes it easy for home vermicomposters.

All you need is a decent-sized container to get started. Chances are, you already have something lying around the house that would work as a free worm bin—maybe an old cooler, a bathtub, or a watering trough?

You want your container to be large enough to hold a decent amount of worms and organic matter, so I'd stick to twenty-gallon-sized or up.

I really like the broken dishwasher I'm using now, since it's small enough to fit into a shady corner behind my barn but large enough to hold plenty of worm food. I can also tip it over if I feel like pouring out all the worm castings and starting anew.

Step 2: Drill Some Drainage Holes

Improper drainage is a worm killer. As you've already learned, one watermelon can lead to the wormpocalypse. Don't make your holes too tiny. Most of your worms won't climb out through the bottom of containers and disappear unless you start feeding them Ipecac or something. In that case, who knows? Just drill a bunch of holes: one-quarter or one-third inch ought to be fine.

Also, when you set up your drainage make sure you have a way to catch the "worm tea" that leaks out of the bottom. Like I said before, that stuff is truly amazing plant food thanks to its broad mix of nutrients and microorganisms. If you're really clever you can nest one container inside another and add a good spigot to the bottom portion rather than just having a single bin with lots of holes in the bottom.

All I did for my dishwasher worm bin is to turn the dishwasher on its back and drill holes at the lowest points. I then lifted it up on some bricks and tucked a container underneath to catch the worm tea. Simple.

Step 3: Find a Top

If you're going to keep your worm bin indoors, you need to make sure flies can't get into it and create a public health crisis in your house. At the same time, the worms need to get enough oxygen, so you can't just snap a tight lid on your container and walk away.

Finally, you don't want your worms to go migrating to your living room one night. If you're using a plastic bin with a matching top, just drill or cut some decent-sized holes in the top, then glue some little pieces of window screening over the holes.

If you have a less-secure home in mind for your wiggly friends, such as my dishwasher, you'll want to keep them someplace where a few runaways or flies don't matter.

Step 4: Fill it Up

Red wigglers love wet, shredded cardboard and paper. What you don't want to do is load up your worm bin with a bunch of rotting food right away. The worms need to get settled. When you add too much food, it rots into a slimy mess rather than being quickly eaten by the worms.

Just find a bunch of paper as noted above—I like to use my bills—and start ripping it up, soak it, squeeze it out after a few minutes, then throw it into the container. Don't forget to add handfuls of soil.

With worm bins, try to avoid adding meat, cheese, oils, and that sort of thing. You'll also want to stay away from food scraps that might be contaminated with a lot of pesticides. You ought to avoid the same! Worms love watermelon rinds, coffee grounds, old salad greens, and even like to hang out in clumps inside of eggshells. They don't seem to like banana peels or citrus, however, so go light or just avoid those until you learn your worms' eating habits.

As you can see, composting with worms doesn't have to be a big deal. You can make your own free worm bin for a minimal amount of effort, and you'll be on the way to vermicomposting greatness.

If you'd like to dig deeper into composting with worms, a great place to start is with Mary Appelhof's classic book *Worms Eat My Garbage*[6]. It's an entertaining and light read that deserves to be on coffee tables across the nation.

And that's all I have to say about worm bins. Build one, chuck compost into it, then harvest incredible compost in both liquid and solid form.

(Dinky! Are you listening??? I'm sorry! I did what you asked! I wrote you into my book! Please stop haunting my dreams!!! Please!!!???)

6. Composting With Melon Pits

A few years ago I read Steve Solomon's *Gardening When It Counts*.[7] In it he mentions in passing that he heard the American Indians used to garden on top of their camp refuse. The remains of feasts, human waste, ashes, crop debris, etc. were tossed in a pit, and plants were grown on top. (This was before the US Fed Gov displaced and killed off many of the natives, of course, so the data on their farming methods are unfortunately limited.)

I haven't been able to nail down where Solomon found his information, unfortunately, but I tried it, and the results were impressive enough that I decided to keep fiddling around and tweaking the method.

Some years ago when I was living in Tennessee, I was plagued by hard, rocky, clay soil. When we had a lot of rain it turned into slick red muck... and when we went without rain for a few weeks, it turned into orange crack-riddled concrete. As we saw in the chapter on sheet mulching, I was able to transform this ground into a great garden, but it didn't happen overnight. Sheet mulching uses a lot of space, is time-consuming, and is a real resource hog. It just takes too long. When I discovered the Native American method it gave me a thought: why not enrich a few small spaces, plant them with squash or melons, then let the vines sprawl around over the grass?

I'm going to tell you a weird story now.

Ever since I was a teenager and first discovered Caribbean cooking while working at the Family Thrift Store (now sadly gone) in one of South Florida's islander-heavy neighborhoods, I've loved goat meat. Particularly spicy curried goat meat.

In Tennessee I had little luck finding goat meat until I met some Ethiopians at church. I told one of them that I was hunting for a good source of goat and they told me they knew just where I could get some: from the Amish. And they told me I could come along if I didn't mind driving them out to a farm they knew.

The thought of traveling to Amish country to buy goat meat with a car full of Ethiopians completely and utterly appealed to me, mostly because I found the entire idea hilarious.

One drizzly winter day we set off together. Since I don't speak Oromo, most of the conversation passed over my head, but the company was still entertaining. Eventually we made it to a farm where the men had bought goat before. Unfortunately we couldn't find the farmer so we drove a little farther down the road to ask directions. At one point we found ourselves watching a group of tall, very dark African men with long poles burning the bristles off a pig over a fire while a row of rosy-cheeked Amish women chopped pork beneath an adjacent tent.

Talk about surreal.

Finally, we found a place that had goats. They were large-bodied, healthy, meat goats, happily playing together in a little field behind a fence. When my friends asked the price, they were told to wait a moment for the owner.

The owner appeared—a teenager, probably fourteen or fifteen. He asked which goats we wanted to buy, and I appealed to my Ethiopian friends for help. They picked one for themselves and one for me.

The taciturn young man nodded at our choices, then took us to a barn decked out for slaughtering. He rapidly slit the goats' throats, hung them up, skinned, and then divided the meat into manageable pieces. While he was doing so, I had a thought: why not save the head and attempt to make goat head soup like I'd had in the Jamaican take-out joint down south? I asked for, and received, the victim's head.

I asked the Ethiopians if they ate goat head soup and they replied in the affirmative. One of them told me "Yes, my wife—she makes a wonderful goat head soup! Ask her about it when you drop us off!"

I did, and she told me just what to do.

"You take the goat head, yes? And you smash it with the knife. Smash it, smash it, smash it, like this," she gestured violently, "Smash it, smash it! Then take onion, pepper, yam... and boil it, and boil it. That's all! Very good!"

When I got home with my cooler of meat my wife was less than impressed by the horrid pieces I'd included in the mix... so she let me know she was less than impressed, then left on a shopping excursion. Alone, I carefully sorted and packed away the pieces in manageable portions, leaving the head on the counter. As I looked at it, it looked back at me. Its mournful eyes dared me to "smash it, smash it." I also noticed the tragicomic way its tongue lolled out of its mouth.

I couldn't do it. I tried to overcome my first-world bias and my cultural proclivities. No dice.

Those eyes... those terrible eyes...

I needed to get rid of the thing before it destroyed my soul. Fortunately I had just finished reading *Gardening When It Counts*, so I knew it could be composted.

And composted it was, along with the bones and organ meat we couldn't manage to cook in a palatable way.

I went out to the garden and started digging pits two to three feet deep into the hard clay on a day when the temperature allowed outdoor work. Despite the ground not being frozen, this still required a pickax and a shovel, making me glad I wasn't double-digging the entire area.

I placed the pits about six feet from each other and threw some ashes in them, along with kitchen scraps, raw manure from a bucket sawdust toilet (more on that in an upcoming chapter!), my wife's failed beef stew, and yes, awful goat parts.

When I filled the dirt back in I made sure the messy stuff was all covered by at least twelve inches or so of soil to keep neighborhood dogs from digging up my hard work (fortunately, the manure seemed to help in that regard). I then made nice mounded tops.

A few months later it was time to plant. I weeded the mounds and the area around them with a hoe, then planted a few sunflower seeds on top of each pit-o-horrid-scariness, and popped in Golden Hubbard squash seeds around those.

For the first couple of weeks the seeds grew normally, and then something happened. Their color rapidly deepened to a rich green, and they sprang into abundant growth. Those plants needed no

additional fertilization and tolerated drought better than the surrounding garden.

Who would've thought that raw human waste, failed stew, and
goat organs would grow some amazing squash? I'll bet you never
read anything about that in *Better Homes and Gardens*. (Inter-
estingly, while researching fellow gardeners' methods of growing
squash, I saw that John Starnes, an urban farmer in Tampa[8], uses
a similar method where he simply buries dog food, which is pretty
close to meat, being intended for consumption by a carnivore, in
his squash mounds and plants on top of that. The concept works!)

After some years of further experimentation I've got a pretty
good thing going. I call them "melon pits" (though I could have
just as easily named them "squash pits," "goat organ repositories" or
"that Native American idea that I ripped off from Steve Solomon),"
and I think they're one of the very best ways to compost items you'd
have a terrifying time trying to compost in a typical backyard bin or
pile.

Melon pits are a safe way to use highly nitrogenous, potentially
dangerous, stinky, yet mineral-rich materials in your gardening.

You can include bones, kitchen scraps, pasta salad, spoiled
meat, livestock carcasses, chunks of wood, road kill, pet droppings,
chicken or any animal manure (just be careful not to get toxic manure—more on that in a future chapter), ashes, pickled pig's feet,
buckets of coffee grounds, rotten fruit, etc. If it's organic and filled
with nutrients, chuck it in.

The method worked well in Tennessee clay and has continued
to work well on my sandy homestead in Florida. I have enough
experience at this point that I can assure you that it can and will
work in your garden as well.

Since the success of my initial goat guts/beef stew/humanure/
ashes melon pits, I've added the additional tweak of burying big
chunks of wood in the holes as well. Buried wood rots and acts like
a wet sponge holding a good volume of water which can keep your
melons or squash going through times of low rainfall.

Are you ready to make your own? Then clean the moldy leftovers out of your fridge, It's time to get started.

Creating a Melon Pit

1. Dig a two to three foot deep hole

You don't want your melon pit to be too shallow. There's nothing
worse than having rotten meat dragged across your yard by marauding raccoons (except for having a recurring dream where you're tied
to a chain link fence and marauding raccoons chew your nose off
while Kate Moss giggles callously at your plight), so make sure the
depth is sufficiently discouraging to animals. It's also important to
make sure the contents are far enough below the natural soil line
that they don't end up getting washed out in a heavy rain. Plant
roots often mine much deeper for nutrients than you'd expect.

2. Dump in chunks of wood and sticks

Again, this is for water retention. Bigger chunks are better. I've
buried fifty pound hunks of logs before. They'll hold water for years
as well as provide a slow release of nutrition. If you only have wood
chips make sure you add lots of something rich in nitrogen along
with them, otherwise the bacteria will take nitrogen to decompose
the carboniferous wood chips, and your plants will suffer accord-
ingly.

3. Dump in dangerous and gross stuff

This can be almost anything you can imagine. I've buried a dead rooster, baked beans, rotten eggs, and even a human placenta. Crazy? No. I did it for science!

4. Cover with loose soil

Depending on your native soil conditions you can either indent your final melon pit or let it become a traditional mound. In Tennessee I planted on mounds; in Florida where drainage is high, I like indentations better. Six to twelve inches of dirt over the top is usually enough to deter roving animals, though not the mocking laughter of Ms. Moss. Adding a few inches of mulch to the top of the melon pit isn't a bad idea, since it will keep out the weeds and keep in extra moisture.

5. Plant (and stand back)

Sprawling vines work the best with this method. You can plant a handful of corn or sunflower seeds in the middle with squash or melons around them, or just plant watermelons… or even plant a tree on top of the melon pit instead. I remember reading of a system of mobile outhouses someone designed for use in Africa. Basically, a deep pit was dug in barren land and an outhouse was placed on top of it. After a year of use, the outhouse was moved and the top of the pit was filled with dirt. Then a tree was planted there. The resulting concentrated fertility allowed the sapling to take hold even under tough conditions. I've done the same with a mulberry tree to great effect.

Some folks worry that somehow the fruit of such a tree—or the lovely Hubbards you'll grow—will be contaminated by what's in the pit. I mean, we all know manure and spoiled meat are dangerous, right? Fortunately, a little bit of scientific inquiry rapidly dispels this notion. There's no way for *E. coli*, a gut bacteria made to live inside nice warm animal and human intestines, can live and travel upwards through a plant. It just doesn't happen. The danger, as we've seen in contaminated spinach recalls, is in raw waste being spattered onto produce that is then consumed. Burying makes this problem no longer a problem, provided you're not in an area that floods. In that case, compost first.

As for why melon pits work well, here's my theory: I believe plants find their own nutrition as they need it. If the roots come in contact with something they don't like, I think they just avoid it. If they find something they like, they go for it.

A couple of years ago I dug about eight pits in my front yard, pouring in whatever manure, ashes, scraps, wood debris, and slaughter wastes that were available at the time.

Since it was chilly out and spring was a ways away, I decided to cover the top of my new hyper-fertile patches with a living mulch. I planted lentils, peas, chickpeas, and fava beans on top of the newly minted melon pits, watered them once, then basically left them alone until the spring. That kept the ground occupied and mostly weed-free until the green carpet was unrolled for the real stars.

Once all the frosts had passed I planted Seminole pumpkins and watermelons in a couple of pits. In some of the other melon pits, I planted perennials, such as figs, mulberries, and guava.

As an additional test, I decided to ignore weeding and watering except when the rain skipped us for a week or more. The plants all did well.

We harvested a good amount of watermelons and Seminole pumpkins. The size of the watermelons wasn't as large as the seed packages advertised, but the fruits were sweet and juicy. The pumpkins produced nice big fruit close to the melon pits but rapidly decreased in vitality and size as they wandered and rooted along their vines farther and farther from their initial planting sites. My front yard has terrible soil; it was obvious that the melon pits had made something possible that would have been impossible otherwise.

As a control group, I also loosened some other patches of soil to a good depth and planted them with watermelon and Seminole pumpkin seeds at the same time I planted my melon pits. Though they were watered regularly, they completely failed to produce a single melon or pumpkin.

If I water and weed my melon pits, the difference is even more remarkable. Even when I almost ignore them, they produce. Pamper them, and you'll be very impressed.

The melon pit system has multiple benefits and no downsides. With melon pits you can:

1. Use organic matter that would normally be too dangerous or "hot" to use.

2. Dispose of "waste" by recycling it into soil fertility.

3. Grow food with very little work.

4. Save water.

5. Concentrate precious fertilizer.

6. Avoid cultivating a large area.

Try melon pits, and see for yourself!

7. Composting Human "Waste"

When they entered the hotel Randy smelled it at once, but not until they reached the second floor did he positively identify the odor. Like songs, odors are catalysts of memory. Smelling the odors of the Riverside Inn, Randy recalled the sickly, pungent stench of the honey carts with their loads of human manure for the fields of Korea. Randy spoke of this to Dan, and Dan said, "I've tried to make them dig latrines in the garden. They won't do it. They have deluded themselves into believing that lights, water, maids, telephone, dining room service, and transportation will all come back in a day or two. Most of them have little hoards of canned foods, cookies, and candies. They eat it in their rooms, alone. Every morning they wake up saying that things will be back to normal by nightfall, and every night they fall into bed thinking that normalcy will be restored by morning. It's been too big a jolt for these poor people. They can't face reality."

Dan had been talking as he packed. As they left the hotel, laden with bags and books, Randy said, "What's going to happen to them?"

"I don't know. There's bound to be a great deal of sickness. I can't prevent it because they won't pay any attention to me. I can't stop an epidemic if it comes. I don't know what's going to happen to them."

—Excerpt from *Alas, Babylon* by Pat Frank[9]

NOTE: The following chapter consists of my own thinking on dealing with human waste and is by no means a blanket permission slip to manage sewage flippantly and give yourself some horrid disease. I am not a doctor or a scientist, let alone an epidemiologist. I'm just a gardener, so proceed at your own risk and don't sue me or my publisher.

No one in their right mind really wants to think much about human waste. In our modern world we've created a vast, complicated, and wasteful system of dealing with our droppings. Countless gallons of water are wasted on "waste," and in many cities the sewer systems and water reclamation plants are overtaxed… yet rather than find better ways to recycle or reuse the offending material, codes ban or simply fail to include environmentally friendly home-based ways of dealing with human manure.

Are you prepared to deal with sewage in a crisis?

What if there isn't a crisis? What if you just want to return your pet's plops to the earth? Is there a better way to manage sewage than throwing it in the trash or flushing it away to be dealt with downstream by some poor guy in Water Management?

Yes! Compost.

After all, we know the stuff grows plants. If you've ever seen the deep green grass over a septic tank, you know what I mean!

I used to have an uncle that ran a truck stop. Every few months, the plumbing would back up, and he'd pump the septic tank out and shoot the disgusting sludge down into a ditch. He told me that an incredible abundance of tomatoes grew there, but he never dared pick any of them.

I wouldn't either.

Manure (raw or composted, human or animal) is an amazing fertilizer. Why not put it to use in a safe manner? If you create a bucket toilet (beyond composting, it's a good idea to have one if you live in a hurricane or flood-prone area), you can collect the odiferous contents and grow food with them.

In China, raw sewage is used directly on food, which is dangerous. It's not that the plants take up the germs—it's that they get splattered. Without boiling, food exposed to raw sewage can literally kill you. However, if that sewage was buried in trenches you could grow tomatoes on top of it and even pick the fruit without washing it (if you wanted to live on the wild side) and you'd probably be fine unless the ground had been flooded at some point and let the sewage come in direct contact with your Better Boys.

So why is the grass greener over the septic tank? Well, everything a person eats during the day isn't able to be used by his body. A lot of very good vitamins and minerals are passed through a person's digestive system either as urine or feces. This, when recycled into the soil, is great food for plants; however, we all know about things such as cholera and *E. coli*. Those scary little bugs are the reason that most people don't use human waste for fertilizer, but they really don't have to be a problem.

There's a classic book by Joseph Jenkins called the *Humanure Handbook*.[10] It's written by a guy who has spent the last few decades defecating into buckets and then composting the results. Not only is he not dead; he apparently has some incredible gardens.

If you do it right, it makes a lot of sense. Why would you go and waste all that potential fertilizer when you don't have to? If you don't own a copy of the *Humanure Handbook*, it's worth purchasing. Find it, buy it. If Western Civilization bites the dust or if you're interested in extreme recycling, this book is invaluable.

A simple sawdust toilet is easy to construct, can be used for years and years, and can be set aside in case of an emergency. If things get really bad, you can use it all the time. Imagine if your well gets shut off because your power's gone and then your generator runs out of gas so you can no longer power the well. If you're forced to rely on rainwater, or carrying buckets from a neighbor's house or pond, you're really not going to want to waste water on a flush toilet. Why not put it to work in your garden?

Before anyone claims this is a suicidal idea, let's think about it a little bit.

Bacteria live in your gut in a nice roughly 98.6 degrees. What do you think life is like for them when they are ejected into the cold, cruel world, and forced to fight with compost pile bacteria, fungi, and critters that just love to eat little bacteria?

They don't do very well. In a year or two, almost all manure is safe to use; even human manure.

Jenkins writes:

> *On several occasions, I have seen simple collection toilet systems (humanure toilets) in which the compost was simply dumped in an outdoor pile, not in a bin, lacking urine*

*(and thereby moisture), and not layered with the coarse or-
ganic material needed for air entrapment. Although these
piles of compost did not give off unpleasant odors (most
people have enough sense to instinctively cover odorous organic material in a compost pile), they also did not necessarily become thermophilic (their temperatures were never
checked). People who are not very concerned about working with and managing their compost are usually willing
to let the compost sit for years before use, if they use it at
all. Persons who are casual about their composting tend
to be those who are comfortable with their own state of
health and therefore do not fear their own excrement. As
long as they are combining their humanure with a car-
bonaceous material and letting it compost, thermophili-
cally or not, for at least a year (an additional year of aging is recommended), they are very unlikely to be creating
any health problems. What happens to these casually constructed compost piles? Incredibly, after a couple of years,
they turn into humus and, if left entirely alone, will simply become covered with vegetation and disappear back
into the earth. I have seen it with my own eyes.*

*A different situation occurs when humanure from a highly
pathogenic population is being composted. Such a population would be the residents of a hospital in an underde-
veloped country, for example, or any residents in a community where certain diseases or parasites are endemic. In
that situation, the composter must make every effort necessary to ensure thermophilic composting, adequate aging
time and adequate pathogen destruction.*

—*The Humanure Handbook*, Chapter 7: Worms and Disease, p. 141[11]

Another thing is, even if you used it fresh (which I am not saying you should do), and you put it around something like a fruit tree and threw some deep mulch over the top of that, how is that going to make you sick? The plant is incapable of taking up *E. coli* through its stem and putting it into the fruit; it just doesn't work that way.

Again, the dangers of *E. coli* are contact related. If someone uses the bathroom in the field and picks some spinach without washing his hands, then somebody in another state or country gets sick. That's not going to happen when you are growing fruit or nuts or other taller crops. You would have to drop an apple on the ground into a wet pile of manure and then eat it.

Like I wrote in the previous chapter on melon pits, I wouldn't use humanure (or other potentially pathogen-bearing composta-bles) any place where you might deal with flooding. You don't want to risk it getting into the water supply or elsewhere in your garden and making you or other folks sick. The safest place for it is buried in the ground or inside a hot compost pile.

Let's make it simple. If a gardener were to dig pits here and there around his fruit trees, or in his food-forest, or even, dare I say it, beneath his garden bed, and then bury waste from a composting toilet system; the chances of him getting sick are next to nil. We live in a culture that is absolutely disconnected from the way nature works. Closing the nutrient loop rather than flushing away organic matter makes a lot of sense.

Of course, if you are really scared of feces and just absolutely terrified that a little poop is going to come and get you in the night and make you ill and die, then stay away from it.

That's fine. Composting droppings isn't for everyone.

I would ask you to consider another fertilizer, however.

Urine.

Did you realize that urine is generally sterile unless a person is dealing with a terrible health problem? Not only that, urine by itself makes a fantastic fertilizer.

I know, the first thing you think about is that time your friend kept peeing on his mom's azalea and it died.

Yes, urine can kill plants. A plant that gets too much may die, but a plant will also die if you dump chemical fertilizer on it. Urine is very rich in nitrogen and also contains a small amount of salts. The trick when using urine as a fertilizer is to dilute it. It can be diluted six or ten parts to one, then used as a foliar feed (applied directly to the leaves) or poured around the base of your trees. Heck, you can just pee around the base of your trees, and they will absolutely love you for it.

Just don't keep peeing (undiluted) on the same spot or on the same plant or you may burn your target.

I once saw a beautiful garden in south Florida that was fertilized with nothing but urine. Every morning, the homeowner would come out, take the previous day's urine and mix it up inside a watering can with water, and then water all the fruits and vegetables.

Obviously, before you eat anything in your salad you'd want to wash it off well if you did that. Peeing on salad greens is… well… rather disgusting. We're not barbarians here.

The takeaway here is that there's an abundant source of fertilizer that comes out of you every single day. It's even been estimated that the amount of urine a person produces in a year is almost exactly the amount of fertilizer that would be required for the food someone eats in a year[12]. Sounds like a pretty good design to me and it sounds like a design we're not taking proper advantage of. For perfectly safe fertilization under duress, urine is the way to go and it is pretty easy.

You can get your wife to pee into a mayonnaise jar, you can pee into a bottle, then you can meet in the garden and pour it out. Take a leak, then pour the leak on the leeks. It's easy!

A few years ago my wife and I actually did an experiment to see if we would be ready for the septic side of a collapse situation (yes, this is what we do with our spare time).

I built a 5-gallon bucket toilet based on the plans in Joseph Jenkins' *Humanure Handbook,* then installed it in the bathroom of our little 3/1 house in Tennessee. For an entire year my family used that toilet and I hauled buckets out of the house in all kinds of weather to a big compost pile at the back of our property. There I'd set up a washing station in the bushes so I could sterilize the buckets after emptying them.

Keep in mind that this was a suburban neighborhood. If this system had stunk at all or attracted flies, etc., we would have been discovered. There wasn't even a fence around my backyard… yet no one ever discovered our experiment. We composted a year's worth of "waste", then used that compost a year later for our gardening.

No one got sick. No one had a problem. No neighbors complained.

That was because we did it right by following Jenkins' system carefully. Do it wrong and you risk African-style cholera epidemics and *E. coli* infections.

There's no need to develop a phobia of feces. They're part of life and they break down rapidly in the soil. In fact, the US Army

Survival Manual only devotes a few sentences to excretion:

> *Do not soil the ground in the camp site area with urine or feces. Use latrines, if available. When latrines are not available, dig "cat holes" and cover the waste. Collect drinking water upstream from the camp site. Purify all water."*

—FM 21-76 US Army Survival Manual

Not scary.

From my research, the biggest problems with feces relate to them getting into water supplies or attracting flies which then become airborne disease vectors. Both of these problems can be eliminated through burying waste in the ground in a proper location. Again, just avoid areas prone to flooding or uphill from wells or springs, and make sure you cover what you leave behind.

My favorite way to deal with sewage is to bury it in melon pits. Secondarily, you can just compost in a big, hot pile with lots of leaves, straw, or wood chips to cover it.

Remember: human waste *can* make you sick if you're foolish, though the fear people have of feces and urine are far beyond its relative danger.

Time is the great healer and composter.

You don't have to deal with a horrible situation like Frank describes in *Alas, Babylon*… yet again, composting is the key.

What About Municipal Waste Composting?

After reading this far, you're probably thinking, "Hey, what about Milorganite™? My Dad/best friend/demon lover/science professor loved using that stuff on their lawn/roses/cabbages/psychedelic cactus collection/zinnias back when I was a kid/teenager/student/princess/guinea pig/ninja/mailman!"

Yes, Milorganite™ is recycled human waste. It's an EPA-approved and inspected product, which makes many feel safe using it.

I'm not so sure.

Whereas Milorganite is likely better than some things you can put on your plants, there are a lot of things that get flushed, drained, and washed into municipal drains. Heavy metals, pharmaceuticals, carcinogens... there's a huge and scary list.

Just imagine what goes down the drain alongside human waste in the average house.

Soaps, urine containing prescription drugs, toilet bowl cleaners, bleach.

Now think about what might wash in from say, a car garage.

Paint, lead, solvents, battery acid, used motor oil.

Or a hair salon.

Dyes, chemicals, shampoos, gossip.

It's crazy to think that they're sorting all that stuff out. Just because they may be contained in low levels doesn't mean that they're safe. Heavy metals like cadmium and arsenic will stick around in your soil a long, long time. I avoid all municipal compost that contains any kind of "biosolids". The bacteria may be contained, but the chemicals aren't safe in my opinion.

If you're going to compost human and pet waste, do it at home, safely!

8. Make Your Own Fish Fertilizer

Remember that old story of the natives teaching the Pilgrims to bury fish beneath their corn plants? It works. That's why "fish emulsion" or "fish fertilizer" is still sold as a common organic fertilizer. Plants love it, and you can make it yourself.

This is a good thing, because fish emulsion is really expensive.

Some time ago my friends Rick and Mart came over for a major yard work day. Both of these guys are pretty hard-core plant geek/survivalist/homesteader types.

When they arrived, Rick said, "Hey… I brought you a little gift from the Caribbean market."

He then proceeded to haul two buckets of nice fresh fish guts and parts from the back of his truck.

I was thrilled. What thoughtful friends I have.

If you have access to fish waste, you can do the same thing I do to compost it into a good liquid fertilizer for your garden. It's easy and it smells incredible.

Here's how I do it.

Step 1: Get a Big Barrel

After this particular project, you're not going to want to use this barrel for anything else, so choose wisely. Try to find a good used 55-gallon drum with a top from the local feed store. Be careful, though: you don't want a drum that used to contain herbicide or pesticide or something nasty. If you can't find one with a top, just find a piece of plywood or something else that will work to keep the smell in and the scavengers out. You also want a lid for this thing to make sure none of the fish turn into undead zombie fish and escape in the night. They'll come in your window, trash your house, and then creep into the refrigerator and go dormant. Then your wife will blame *you* for the mess and the smell. Don't let that happen.

Step 2: Throw in the Guts!

Go ahead and imagine you're Jackson Pollock (Get it? Pollock? Like the fish!) as you splatter fish guts into the bottom of your drum.

Step 3: Add Some Carbon!

We all know about the whole boring C:N part of composting, right? That is, for nitrogenous material, it helps to add some carbon so the microorganisms get plenty to snack on as they break down a pile. You can do the same thing with your fish fertilizer. I like adding sawdust or wood chips. You could also just add shredded paper or straw, or skip this step altogether. The idea is just to give a little more balance to your fertilizer. We're anaerobic composting here. It may be a nasty wharf-scented slop, but it's still compost.

Step 4: Pour Some Sugar On Me

Actually, we're pouring sugar in the bucket of horrors, not onto our lover. This adds even more carbon, plus gives the bacteria a nice head rush. I have a gallon of livestock molasses I use for projects like this (and on my oatmeal). I like to imagine it has more micronutrients in it, though I have no idea. Drop in a few sloppy blubs.

Now… there's just one more step to do. I call it "Step 5." And… here it is:

Step 5: Make It Into Soup

Grab your hose and add a generous amount of water to the mix. Say 25 gallons or more. That's enough to keep everything nice and wet while it rots down.

Easy! Now comes the hard part… waiting. Some folks will recommend you stir this fetid elixir now and again. I think that's a good idea, since it gets some oxygen in there and mixes everything up. Just know this: eventually, it will rot down. Bit by bit, the yuckiness will subside and you'll end up with a rich, fish-sauce-scented fermented brew that plants adore. The secret is time.

As a final note, this mixture is loved by more than just plants. The first time I made fish fertilizer I had vultures land in my yard within an hour of starting the project.

One other thing: depending on the amount of fish guts added, this could be strong stuff. Make sure you thin it out before applying to plants.

Also, don't use this stuff on your salad greens. It's better and safer as an amendment or foliar feed for plants you're not going to immediately put in your mouth.

To foliar feed, simply pour a few cups of fish fluid through a strainer (coffee filters work too slowly; an old T-shirt is better) into a plant sprayer, then fill the rest of your sprayer with water. It's hard to figure out how concentrated your emulsion really is so go easy at first.

Though the process is stinky, I'd much rather feed ripe fish to my plants than have them end up in a landfill. You're turning trash into treasure, even if the process is a little less than savory.

And you know, if you don't feel like making fish emulsion, just go ahead and bury the carcasses in a melon pit.

Or beneath your corn.

9. A Mournful Tale of Manure

When my blackberry leaves started curling up into deformed fractals, I thought perhaps they'd received too much nitrogen. Then my wife's newly transplanted tomatoes started doing the same. *Probably a virus*, I thought. Then the beans did it. And an eggplant. But when my mulberry tree also joined the club, I realized something more sinister might be in play.

Google searches and calls to friends revealed nothing—until I happened to come across an article in a British newspaper about a community garden struck with the same plight. Once I found one article—and a suspect—it was easy to find a lot more of the same.

What had been killing my plants and those of my fellow gardeners across the Atlantic?

Apparently, cow manure! You know, that wonderful, plant-healthy, organic standby to chemical fertilizers. But it wasn't the manure itself that was to blame—it was a persistent herbicide inside it.

Had that killed my garden? I needed to know.

The previous fall I had indeed gotten some manure. In fact, I bought a double load of good rotted stuff from a local cattle farmer, spread it around my trees and plants, and dug it into the lovely new vegetable beds I constructed for my wife.

After identifying the likely suspect, I realized I'd done something terrible: I'd also shared some of my pile with a fellow Master Gardener. If her plants were showing the same symptoms...

Breathlessly, I picked up the phone and gave her a call.

"Jo? This is David. How is your garden doing?"

"Fine," she replied, then paused. "Actually... my tomatoes are really curling up and twisting... I have no idea what's wrong with them... I've grown them in these beds for years and never seen anything like this..."

"Did you use my manure on them...?

"Yes, and..."

The call confirmed my fears. With many apologies, I revealed my suspicions and decided it was time to dig deeper into the steaming pile of deadly droppings.

Many herbicides break down rapidly. The much-maligned (probably for good cause) RoundUp™ is a contact-based killer and (allegedly) disintegrates rapidly into the environment under normal conditions. At the very least, it doesn't keep killing plants for a long period after application. But the stuff I had used to unknowingly poison my plants was different. It was a persistent hormone-based toxin that could be sprayed on a field, eaten by an animal, digested, excreted, composted in a heap... and still kill plants.

The butler in this mystery, it seems, was Aminopyralid, sold by the trade name Grazon™.

Created by Dow AgroSciences, it specifically targets a variety of non-grass species by inhibiting their cell stacking functions, causing gross deformations and plant death. It stays in the soil for an unreasonably long period of time (estimates vary; I've come across a range from one to five years!) and does not break down under composting.

If a cow munches hay harvested in a field where Aminopyralid has been sprayed, their manure becomes a plant killer instead of a plant feeder. The normal ecological cycle has been disrupted. Worse than that, it can be found in bales of straw, bagged manure and compost, and it's almost impossible to track the supply chain back to who sprayed what... where... and when.

Most gardeners who lose their plants are likely to assume their thumb wasn't green enough—not that they've been poisoned by industrial agriculture! As a person sick of genetically-modified foods, toxic pesticides, and heavy metal-containing sewage being passed off as a safe "biosolid" fertilizer, having my own plots raped by the machine was particularly infuriating.

The story doesn't end there, however. Armed with a bunch of new information, I called the farmer who had sold me the manure. Long a fixture in the area where I live, he was horrified to hear that his manure had caused me to lose my plants, though he told me no one else had called to say they'd had any problems (likely because they didn't know what did it).

I asked if he'd used anything on his fields the previous year that might have carried through his animals and into the manure pile. "Just a new herbicide recommended for pigweed... it worked great... and it's safe for the cows to eat," he told me. I asked if he knew what it was called... and he told me he wasn't sure, but he'd let me know. I gave him my e-mail.

A few days later, true to his word, the farmer sent me an e-mail. In it, he told me the substance's name and sent a link to its ingredients.

Aminopyralid. Case closed.

My cattle-farming friend had no idea the toxin could continue downstream and, in fact, most farmers don't. Universities and extension offices actively recommend the substance as an excellent weed control. And it works. Too well.

That year as I looked across the empty beds of black soil that should have been teeming with lush green life, I was saddened by the loss of my crop.

I dug up the blackberries, washed their roots and planted them in new spots, then scraped the manure away from all my trees. For most of them, it was too late. Some of the trees, years later, are still stunted and really just need to be pulled up. On the very tiny upside, I did get a refund from the farmer.

With Aminopyralid and other long-term herbicides, organic gardeners like you and me are getting the shaft. The chances of banning a moneymaking substance like this are minimal. Those of us who wish to grow things naturally and without poisons have to be savvy, sharp, and a step ahead. Keep your eyes open. If an age-old garden amendment like cow manure isn't safe, who knows what is?

I have a sneaking suspicion God allowed this garden writer to lose a few plants so I can save many others from the same experience. If that's the case, so be it… but I'll never forgive the folks at Dow AgroSciences for trashing my garden.

The big thing that gets me: because of this stuff, we're basically having to throw manure away. That's insane!

This last year a friend told me "Hey Dave, I got a source for lots of rotted horse manure!"

"Do you know if they only graze on that property, and if that property is sprayed, and if they use hay brought in from elsewhere?"

"No."

"Then it isn't safe. Thanks, but no thanks."

Organic gardeners like my friend love manure; yet if you use it wrong, you may destroy all you've worked for.

Using manure in your gardens is a great way to direct compost; however, I want you to do it safely. If you're raising your own animals or composting your own excrement, great. If not—beware. Aminopyralids aren't the only villain. We'll cover more later in this chapter.

Now let's dig deeper into manure.

Why Use Manure?

The earth was designed to be a self-perpetuating system. Many animals feed off plants, which in turn feed off animals, both on their manure and eventually on their bodies when they die.

As animals graze, they pick up plenty of nutrients, and what they can't use during the course of the day gets excreted. Both urine and manure are good for gardening but if you've ever tried to get a goat to pee into a mayonnaise jar, you know why farmers usually just collect manure for their plots. (Note: stable bedding is loaded with urine and is great for the compost heap).

Using animal droppings for farming also makes sense because it closes the nutrient loop and reincorporates fertility into the soil, rather than disposing of it off-site.

For most of recorded history, man has used manure to nourish

his crops. Unfortunately, that usage fell drastically with the advent
of the tractor and the rise of chemical fertilization. It's a lot easier to
handle dry granules with perfect NPK ratios than it is to collect and
distribute manure. On a small family farm, where you might have
chickens, goats, a cow or even a horse, using manure is easy... but
it's not so easy on large farms that are growing monoculture crops
without the use of animals.

Unlike chemical fertilizers, manure contains a broad range of
nutrients. It also contains organic matter and a range of microorganisms that improve the tilth of the soil as well as its biodiversity.

I once saw a backyard where a couple had once dropped a load
of cow manure to incorporate into their gardens as needed. The
surprising thing was that the grass where they'd originally thrown
their manure off the trailer was still green and lush years after the
manure had been used up.

That's good stuff.

What Manure?

This is where things get a little more complicated. The gardener has
a variety of manures available for his fertilizing arsenal: you have to
determine which makes sense in your garden. Some are usually too
"hot" to use right away, like cow, bat, or chicken wastes. Others are
filled with weed seed, like horse droppings. And others, like humanure (as we've seen) need to be handled carefully to avoid contact
with pathogens.

The good news: composting fixes almost everything. If you're
not sure if your manure is too hot, compost it (or bury it in a melon
pit). Waiting allows some of the nitrogen to dissipate, and it kills
off pathogens. A few months is usually good enough, but if you're

paranoid about germs, two years is the magic number for complete safety.

Goat and rabbit manure are super special because you can apply them directly to the garden without having to worry about burning your plants. I use the manure from our rabbits around my favorite plants, and they never get burned. This stuff is garden gold, and I have the peppers to prove it.

Though chicken manure sometimes gets a bad rap for being a garden killer, I've also found that side-dressing plants with a dusting of dry chicken manure works well. Just go light. I went a little nuts one year and roasted some of my kale. If your plants turn yellow and brown then you're doing it wrong.

Whatever manure you have access to, chances are there's a use for it in your garden, unless... well, you'd better just keep reading.

The Bad News On Manure

I used to work at an advertising/media agency back before I discovered how great it was to own my own business.

One day my friend Will and I were talking about some scandal in which yet another respected leader was caught directly lying to people. After years of writing advertising and discovering how salespeople and marketers would toss the truth under a bus in a heartbeat if there was money involved, we were both pretty fed up with fake, and this was a crystallizing moment.

Will shook his head and muttered to himself.

"Everything is bull–! Everything."

He looked up at me, eyes burning with tortured insight, face reminiscent of an ancient mystic or half-starved monk.

"It's true, isn't it? Everything is bull–! Everything."

Unfortunately, in this fallen world, that's basically true. Yet unlike cow manure, the "bull" we're subjected to on a daily basis isn't even useful for fertilizing.

Enough philosophizing. So why do I bring up this conversation? Because manure from off your farm (and probably on as well, unless you're being very careful) may be contaminated with a variety of nasty things you don't want in your garden... just as I shared in the case of Aminopyralids earlier.

It's ironic that the excrement itself is the least offensive part of manure... but there you go.

What contaminants? Try these on for size:

1. Heavy metals

There's arsenic in some factory chicken feed. There's also a variety of other heavy metals that are in a lot of commercially produced composts, thanks to "green" composting programs that recycle sewer sludge into fertilizer. Though on the surface, it seems like a great idea, but the reality is that a lot of pollutants end up in the sewers as we saw in the previous chapter. As mentioned before, if you buy any bagged composts, manures, or fertilizers, you could be adding a nice dose of poison to your soil. If you have a local factory chicken operation or dairy that gives away manure, just skip it.

2. Pharmaceuticals

Animals are given a wide range of drugs, some of which fail to break down quickly and are passed into the animal's waste. You probably don't want these in your garden.

3. Pesticides

Oh yes, let's not forget these. Fields are sprayed with a bunch of junk to kill pests. Some of these fields are growing crops that are then fed to animals, and—you guessed it—it comes on through.

4. Antibiotics

Now this isn't cool. The soil relies on an intricate balance of competing and cooperating species. When you dump antibiotics into the ground, you kill off some organisms and pave the way for others to become dominant. You also increase the chances of "superbugs" arriving through adaptation to the toxic conditions. Since a lot of animals are kept in tight quarters under harsh conditions, massive amounts of antibiotics are given to them, and those medications come on through.

5. Herbicides

As you read before, this set of chemicals produces the most drastic effects. They can literally destroy your entire garden in days, and they're now everywhere. Thanks to Agricultural Extensions and their unholy alliance with companies like Dow AgroSciences, herbicides are regularly recommended and applied to fields where animals graze. They stick around for a long, long time... many times for years.

This is absolute madness.

A friend once wrote me and said "I asked the Ag extension people and they said to not worry about herbicides in their compost, it's all gone by the time it's available."

That's not true at all. I responded to her with this:

"Do *not* trust the Ag extension. They're totally wrong. Some of these toxins can and do persist in manure and other composts for up to five years. Remember: they are a distribution point for information that sells product. When I first wrote on the problem in my garden for them, they wouldn't allow me to mention companies or brand names, even though the info is out there. Just one of the reasons I dropped my Master Gardener title."

Yep. I left the Master Gardeners for the same reason I left the advertising industry. At some point you just get sick of covering for liars and people that don't give a darn about the facts.

Unfortunately, most of the manure stream has been poisoned with these chemicals at this point.

How To Make Sure Manure Won't Kill Your Garden

It's a bummer way to end this chapter, but here's my recommendation: don't import manure for your garden if:

1. The source farm isn't organic

2. The animals are eating imported feed/hay or living in imported bedding straw

3. The animals are treated with chemical de-wormers/antibiotics/etc.

4. A bagged manure/compost contains "biosolids"

As you'll quickly see from that list it's basically impossible to meet those criteria. Yet if you don't, you're running the risk of poisoning your ground. It's just not safe to add manure anymore unless you *know* it's safe.

The best bet is to raise your own animals and use their manure… or use your own manure.

Manure is indeed one of the best fertilizers for your garden.

It's just too bad we've poisoned the living daylights out of everything. Watch your back.

The First Line of Defense

Don't bring manure, compost, straw, or grass clippings onto your property. Trust no one except people that don't feed their animals *any* purchased hay and who you are sure do *not* spray their fields with anything.

This is the only way to be completely sure your garden won't get whacked. Look, I'm not hyper cautious, but this is deadly stuff, and it sticks around in the ground. It's been years since I got hit and many of my perennials never recovered. The supply chains are really long. It's really hard to find out where hay and straw originally came from.

Chances are, a lot of it is being sprayed.

Aminopyralids don't hurt grasses, so they're often used on wheat, corn, grains, and pastures. In the name of convenience and saving time, they're poisoning the supply chain for organic farmers. Once you know about the existence of these long-term pesticides and the range of their use, you'll look sideways at a lot of amendments that used to be perfect for your garden. The game has changed. Don't get nailed.

The Second Line of Defense

If you've got access to a pile and want to know if it's contaminated, you can get it tested if you're willing to part with a few hundred bucks.

If not, you can take some manure, mix it with some dirt, and transplant a tomato seedling into it. Plant a few beans at the same time. Those two plants are good "canaries," since they become obviously affected quicker than other veggies.

A couple of weeks after germination, if the beans are developing a second and third set of leaves without any obvious distortion and if the tomato plant is growing normally, you're probably good. Unless some other part of the pile contained manure that was excreted after the animal ate a little hay from a sprayed field, then you might still be screwed.

Really, is it worth it? You decide. For me, the answer is no. I've been down that road once and have a thousand dollars worth of dead plants and lost crops to prove it.

But there's the test, should you choose to take the risk. If there's any kind of weirdness in the growth of your beans or tomatoes, run away. Fast.

The Third Line of Defense

When I had to pick up the pieces after the Manurepocalypse, I had a second conversation with Jo, and she told me that the tomato plants she'd spread ashes around were doing better than the ones without ashes.

Ah-ha! Could carbon be the answer?

I knew that activated charcoal was a great way to soak up toxins, so I burned piles of sticks into ashes and charcoal, then dug those into all my affected beds. I also read that soil organisms can break Aminopyralids down over time, so I added a lot of dirt from my chicken run, knowing that it was highly "alive" stuff.

It helped, but it was too late for the spring crops. They all kicked off. The next plants did better, but not perfect. Two years later I was still seeing pockets of weirdness here and there in my beds.

I wondered if perhaps composting could knock out this stuff, since it's great at removing a lot of other issues. The answer is no. Basically, your best bet is to mix charcoal (Not briquettes, moron! No, Lobo! *No*!!!) and some dirt into your beds, and hope that after a few years all the effects are gone, or just start over with new dirt or new beds.

It's that nasty.

The Final Scoop

I'm going to say this again with an exclamation point:

Don't bring manure, compost, straw, or grass clippings onto your property. Trust no one except people that don't feed their animals *any* purchased hay and who you are sure do *not* spray their fields with anything. This is the only way to be completely sure your garden won't get whacked!

And one more time, with three exclamation points:

Don't bring manure, compost, straw, or grass clippings onto your property. Trust no one except people that don't feed their animals *any* purchased hay and who you are sure do *not* spray their fields with anything. This is the only way to be completely sure your garden won't get whacked!!!

If you do, don't say I didn't warn you. For preppers, organic gardeners, and farmers, one bad run-in with manure can wipe you out. Please don't take the risk. If you really want to use manures, get it from your own animals provided you don't feed them any outside hay. You can also compost your own manure, Joseph Jenkins-style.

Otherwise, you're treading on dangerous, poisoned ground.
Of course, another thing you can do is lobby against this stuff.
Good luck with that.

10. Grow Your Own Compost

Buy this, buy that. Then get some of this, and a handful of these, then some more of that, and a few of those...

Gardening can get expensive if you do it the normal way.

Let's run the rough numbers on building a four-by-eight foot bed:

3 eight foot cedar boards: $65.00

8 Bags of mushroom/cow manure/garden soil or other bagged compost: $40.00

5 six-packs of vegetable transplants: $15.00

1 box of screws: $4.00

TOTAL: $124.00

Now really, $124.00 isn't a bad price to pay. Over time, a garden bed will pay for itself in homegrown organic produce, provided you don't count in the labor costs. (If you do, all is lost... so don't. There will be tears.) However, what if you didn't need to spend all that money? If you wanted to, you could give up the Most Noble Constrained Order of Raised Beds and just double-dig. You could also grow your own transplants from seed, which is another money saver.

Beyond that, there's the compost. And that's the real focus of this book: compost!

So, how can you get more compost?

Thus far we've talked about scrounging for anything and everything, including meat, manure, failed cooking experiments, and fish guts... yet what if that isn't enough?

I daresay very few of us create enough compost to meet our gardening needs, particularly if we're gardening intensively in beds. Most gardeners simply throw in some yard waste and whatever comes out of the kitchen, creating a measly few buckets of good stuff in a year. More enterprising composters (like you and I, O Reader) will wander their towns and neighborhoods in search of piles of grass clippings, rotten straw, manure, and even rotten vegetables from local dumpsters.

The ultimate in composting, however, is to grow your own from scratch. Let's take a look at how this can be done at home.

Grow Your Own Compost

John Jeavons, in his book *How to Grow More Vegetables*,[13] urges gardeners and farmers to devote 60 percent of their growing space to compost crops, i.e., high carbon crops. Basically you're planning in lots of greenery that can be composted and fed to next year's gardens. By doing this on a large enough scale you can eliminate the need to buy compost.

Just because these crops are ultimately destined for the compost bin, it doesn't mean they have to be just for that. Often these carboniferous compostables are calorie sources as well. If you're growing a bed of kale, you don't really get much compost out of it at the end of the season. The same goes for many of our favorite edibles, such as bush beans, cauliflower, and peppers. These produce are good fare for the table but not for the compost pile.

You'd likely have to grow five thousand carrots to get enough tops to make a bucket of finished compost. That's just silly. You're looking for plants that produce a lot of biomass.

Another thing to consider: what if you simply grow plants as green manure? No compost pile required! Just throw seeds around, and when the plants get to a good height, usually right before they set seed, chop them down in place or till them under. You're instantly adding the organic matter of the plant tops. And even better, the roots beneath the ground rot and provide more organic matter along with loose soil.

Let's take a look at some of some tried-and-true good guys, starting with the edibles.

Edible Crops for Composting

NOTE: I live in a subtropical climate so not all of these plants will work for you, but most of them probably will. Try some and see... and always be on the lookout for plants that get nice and big in a short period of time.

Amaranth

Amaranth is an ancient grain crop that isn't really a grain at all. It's a spinach relative with prolific growth potential. Some varieties will get as tall as you; others are more diminutive. All of them have edible greens and leaves. Be careful when you compost amaranth, however, as it's a prolific self-seeder. If you don't want it forever, cut it before the seed heads mature!

Autumn Olive, Goumi Berry and Sea Buckthorn

Autumn olives are small trees that bear an edible cherry-like fruit and fix nitrogen. They're a scrappy and somewhat invasive tree once planted at old mines to help control erosion and restore the soil.

Goumi berries are a cousin of autumn olive with deliciously tart and easy-to-grow fruit, and like peanuts, beans, and peas they fix nitrogen and improve soil.

Finally, the popular Sea Buckthorn checks in as another nitrogen-fixing shrub with edible berries. Bonus: it can stand extreme cold *and* it's loaded with antioxidants, making it incredibly healthy for you.

Though the trimmings are woody on these trees/shrubs they can be used as the base for a compost heap. You can also plant these species close to a tree you'd like to feed. Every time you prune them back, just chuck the branches at the base of the other tree. They'll also drop some nitrogen off their roots from the stress and that new fertility can be taken up by their companions.

Beans, Peanuts and Peas

Peanuts fix nitrogen, as do beans and peas. Soybeans are commonly cropped in cornfields to add back some of the nitrogen taken by the grain harvest. Locally, there's a farmer who grows Southern peas between his harvests of corn and watermelons. Because of their relationship with nitrogen-fixing bacteria, beans, peas, peanuts, and other legumes are excellent soil-repairing edibles. They literally pull fertilizer out of thin air, plus you can eat them. Though many beans aren't particularly tall, their ability to make fertilizer beneath the soil makes them a great compost-in-place plant.

Buckwheat

Want to eat delicious, hearty pancakes for minimal work? Buckwheat is your crop!

Though it's not a true grain and has nothing to do with wheat, buckwheat is an easy-to-grow grain-like crop. Buckwheat grows rapidly and produces a crop in about two and a half months.

How does it fix soil? Buckwheat makes a wonderful green manure or compost pile stuffer. Toss the seed around, let it grow for a few weeks, then till it under. Because it grows thickly, you can also use buckwheat as a "smother crop" to shade out and kill undesirable weeds.

As an additional bonus, buckwheat's abundant flowers feed the bees and other pollinators.

Corn

Grain corn—particularly the large dent varieties—produce a lot of biomass in a season, plus you get to eat grits. Corn stalks take a while to break down, but they will compost eventually. The grain is good for grits, corn bread, and feeding your animals.

Daikon Radish

Daikon radishes are hole-punching machines that readily open up compacted soil. Their use as a soil-building no-till crop was popularized by the late Masanobu Fukuoka. Plant these radishes, and let them grow. They'll drive their taproot deep into the earth, overwinter, then bloom and die the next year, leaving loose, organic matter-rich soil in their wake. You can also eat them before that point, of course, and still get the benefit of their soil-opening ability.

Fava Beans

No matter where you are in the US, you can grow fava beans. In much of the nation you can even grow these cold-hardy nitrogen fixers during the winter. They grow into bushes a few feet tall and yield edible seeds, either as immature green beans (shelled) or as mature dry beans.

Moringa

Moringa trees grow very quickly and also have serious fertilizing power. They can be chopped over and over again, and the wood and leaves rot quickly. I can't confirm this, but I've also heard their leaves contain a growth stimulant that increases the vitality of other plants. Unfortunately, if you live north of USDA growing zone 9, growing moringa will be tricky.

Mesquite

If you live in the arid southwest, you're familiar with mesquite trees. They have the potential to become a big pain in the neck, since they fix nitrogen, seed prolifically, plus tend to form dense stands of trees where nothing else can grow. That said, the seed pods are edible and easy to harvest, plus the trees provide shade for more tender plants. Though the trees are tough to cut down, the wood is excellent for smoking and wood crafts. Finally, their nitrogen-fixing ability means they also repair the soil as they grow. If you live where they'll grow, it's worth keeping a few around for easy calories and extra biomass.

Mustard

Mustard? What? As in the salad green/condiment?

Yep. Not only does mustard grow quickly into a large-leafed plant (make sure you buy the big types), making it a good source of rapid biomass or green manure, it can repel or even kill nematodes. Anything that kills nematodes is great in my book. It's also tasty as a cooked green. Win.

Pigeon Peas

Pigeon peas are a tall tropical perennial legume that both fixes nitrogen and produces a lot of good growth in a season. You can often get the dry seeds (sold as food) from Indian or Caribbean groceries. In most of the US, pigeon peas won't produce a crop before frosts take them to the ground, but they do grow quickly and will enrich the ground and your compost pile. If you live in USDA Zone 9 or south, they're a highly productive source of protein-rich peas. The woody stems are quite hard (this is actually a short-lived tree, not a vegetable) and can be used for rocket stove fuel or as stakes for your garden.

Small Cereal Grains

These are recommended by Jeavons with cereal rye being the peak, thanks to its tall stalks and extensive root system. I'm not a fan of eating grain (though I have a soft spot for dent corn), but if you've got blank earth that needs cover, hungry chickens, a need for compost—or all three, it's hard to beat these grasses. Let them dry down in the field and scythe them down when brown to mix with greens in the compost pile (or throw them on the ground!) or turn them under while they're still green to give the ground a burst of quick-rotting fertility. Alternately, you can simply crop grain down to the ground when it goes to seed, then throw the resultant straw and seeds to your chickens, or, even better, let the chickens roam over it and pick their own. They'll turn the stalks into compost and transmogrify the grain into eggs.

Sunflowers

Sunflowers are beautiful and edible, plus good for compost. When I've grown them I've generally had problems with insects infesting the seed heads; however, you can simply throw the heads to your chickens or hang them up for wild birds to eat. Your feathered friends don't mind the grubs and weevils!

Tall varieties of sunflowers are excellent for compost, and they also add cheer to any yard or garden.

Sweet Potatoes

You might not think of sweet potatoes as a compost crop but they do make a vast profusion of vines that can be added to compost piles or thrown around the base of trees to be composted where they fall. Just be aware: sweet potatoes are really good at rooting themselves and taking over unless the vines are either dried out or have been killed by cold.

Non-edible Compost Crops

Comfrey

Comfrey is the king of permaculture plants. Organic gardeners and herbalists swear by the stuff, both as a fertilizer and as a health supplement and bone healing herb.

As a fertilizer, comfrey is particularly high in potassium. It also contains a range of other nutrients and micro nutrients, thanks to its extraordinary root system. If you live in a more tropical area comfrey may fail you, but through most of the country comfrey is almost a weed. As a bonus, it's perennial!

To make a liquid fertilizer from comfrey, chop off the top of a plant and throw the leaves in a bucket. Cover with water; they rot quickly. When you have a nice liquid, water whatever plants need a boost.

Duckweed and Azolla

Most everyone has encountered duckweed at some point. It's a tiny floating plant that has the ability to rapidly cover a pond in a short period of time. Pond owners often hate it for that reason, but their pain is our gain.

Azolla is a similar plant in its growth habit; however, it's a nitrogen-fixing fern. I have a friend who has a few long, shallow ponds that are completely covered with duckweed and azolla. He regularly goes out with a skim net and fills buckets with this dynamic duo, then feeds them both to his plants and to his bins of composting worms.

Both duckweed and azolla are filled with protein, and protein equals nitrogen!

Bonus: they can be used to feed your ducks.

Mexican Sunflowers

Mexican sunflowers, also known as *Tithonia diversifolia* (don't get them confused with *Tithonia rotundifolia*, the annual Mexican sunflower) are fast-growing perennials that tower overhead. Mine reach twenty feet every year then burst into bloom in the fall. You can cut them over and over again and reap the benefits in the form of crumbly compost. For gardeners in USDA zone 8 and warmer, *Tithonia diversifolia* will grow back from the ground provided the soil doesn't freeze. It grows really, really fast.

Mexican sunflowers are a very good source of phosphorus as well as other nutrients. You can chop them down multiple times every year, and they'll just keep growing back. They're also beautiful in the fall when they bloom. As a bonus, the butterflies and pollinators love them.

Water Hyacinth

Water hyacinth is in fact edible but I'm including it here since most folks don't and won't eat it. This incredibly invasive plant is the bane of states with warm water and lots of rivers, canals, lakes, and ponds.

Its population can double in less than two weeks, and it grows and grows and grows until it covers the entire surface of the water. Most government eradication programs that I'm aware of use herbicides to kill water hyacinth; however, there's a much better way to deal with this very productive plant: compost it!

Since water hyacinth is a floating plant that can't live outside of the water, you can drag it out and pile it up for an instant compost pile. It will rot in place and make great humus for your garden. It can even be deliberately grown as compost fodder in an old swimming pool or pond set aside for the purpose. Toss wheelbarrows of water hyacinth around the base of your fruit trees, in the rows of your garden, add them to sheet mulches, or put them in your compost bin.

More On Nitrogen Fixers

George Washington Carver's work in agriculture has filtered down into mainstream culture, spawning lots of jokes about the crazy products he created from peanuts… though most people don't really know *why* he planted peanuts.

Carver's experiments with crop rotation were geared towards restoring the depleted soils left behind by years of cotton farming. The reason peanuts played heavily into this plan? Nitrogen!

Like many members of the bean and pea family, peanuts have a special relationship with certain soil bacteria that allow them to "fix nitrogen." Basically, these microbes live on the roots of certain plants, enjoying the sugars exuded, and paying for their rent by taking nitrogen from the air and converting it into a form that can be used by plants in the soil.

In its simplest form, when you plant plants that add nitrogen to the soil, you're fertilizing from *thin air*. That alone is a great reason to add these powerhouses to your garden plans, even if you don't use them to make candy, ink, shampoo, margarine, rubber, ropes, cloth, deodorant, etc.

Adding Nitrogen Fixers to Your Garden

Are you growing beans or peas? I touched on this before, so you already know why: growing beans and peas will add nitrogen to your soil. To utilize the power of nitrogen fixers in a really cheap way over a large area, just buy cheap bags of beans, raw peanuts, peas, and lentils from the supermarket and scatter them across unused beds and newly tilled ground.

In the summer, I stick to warm weather nitrogen fixers like southern peas, limas, kidney beans, peanuts, etc. In the fall, winter, and spring, I plant lentils, chick peas, fava beans, and dry peas.

It doesn't matter if these plants ever produce anything: they keep the ground covered and alive while adding valuable nitrogen. To get the best bang for your buck, you can snip them off at ground level or till them under before you plant your next crop and let the nitrogen-nodule bearing roots rot beneath the ground. Yanking them out removes too much.

Though it's disputed, I believe that nitrogen fixers feed the plants around them even without being tilled under. That's why I often mix lentils and peas in with my cabbages and scatter beans around my fruit trees.

Using Nitrogen Fixers in Your Orchard or Food Forest

When permaculture gurus plan a "food forest," they make liberal use of nitrogen fixing trees and shrubs. By adding these fertilizer producers, they can feed the young food-producing trees near them without adding extra chemical or organic fertilizers.

Basically, they're growing fertilizer in place.

In my food forest, I'm growing some plants of questionable nitrogen-fixing ability (honey locust [*Gleditsia triacanthos*] and candlestick cassia [*Senna alata*]) along with proven nitrogen fixers like *Leucaena leucocephala*, pigeon pea, coral bean, *Enterolobium* (spp.), mimosa trees (*Albizia julibrissin*) and multiple varieties of *Elaeagnus*. If I remember, I also throw around southern peas and other annual nitrogen fixers when I break up an area of ground or plant new trees. There are a lot of options on this front, especially if you're not trying to grow anything edible. Lupins, vetch, velvet beans, clover… there are plenty to choose from.

Many nitrogen-fixing plants are also fast growers, which means they can be cut regularly and thrown around more important plants (such as your apple tree) as mulch, or simply composted and fed to the soil in needy places.

Potential Problems

One problem you may have when you look for nitrogen-fixing trees: many of the very best have been added to lists as "invasive" species. I don't fear invasive species since I'm an active gardener, but I know a lot of people that find them terrifying, including the USDA and native plant societies.

If it's a variety that makes tons of seeds and dumps them all over, you can cut off the blooms when they form. If it's a species that climbs far up into your neighbor's trees, keep it from doing that. (Kudzu was originally planted as a great nitrogen fixer, and look how helpful it's been!)

Nitrogen fixers are the elite forces of the Plant Kingdom. They were designed to take care of themselves, repair the soil, and pave the way for less-hardy species. Remember this, or they may eat your garden.

Just be smart and let the plants work for you. If you incorporate nitrogen fixers into your planning, it means you'll have a lot less need for fertilizer. Plus, you'll also get some great food from some species.

Chopping and Dropping

Though John Jeavons' *Grow Biointensive*™ method of gardening uses rye, fava beans, and cornstalks as additives for carefully constructed compost piles, there's an easier way to convert the biomass on your property into soil-building humus. It's called the "chop 'n' drop" method. You'll see this used extensively in permaculture, as it mimics the way a forest floor is built, just in fast-forward mode.

Say you've just planted an apple tree and would like to give it a good start in life. You might mulch it with some straw or wood chips when you plant, but at the same time you plant, you could also plant a few trees or shrubs near that tree that will grow quickly and provide mulch and nutrition for your fruit tree.

In my food forest I plant lots of nitrogen fixers, moringa trees, Mexican sunflowers, and other sources of biomass. Throughout the year I'll chop and drop their branches and leaves to the ground around my fruit and nut trees. When you do this you take advantage of the nutrition those plants have taken up from the soil, and you also keep a layer of mulch going around your more precious trees.

The same can be done with weeds! Got a luxuriant patch of ragweed, dog fennel, pokeweed, or other tall and vigorous weed species?

Grab your hand sickle and chop down a few bundles of biomass to spread around the base of your apple. Don't bother composting tall weeds in a pile, shredding it with a lawn mower, or, God forbid, burning it down. Let them grow tall, then feed them to something else that will eventually feed you.

Growing compost can be as complex as building a pond for aquatic plants, or as simple as letting the weeds grow all summer and then piling them up in the fall. The only limit is your imagination.

11. Dealing With Stupid Worthless Trees

"I'd love to garden, but I've got all these huge hackberries, see, and they shade everything..."

"Man, if I was going to put that acre into production, I'd have to get rid of all those laurel cherries and other trash trees..."

"We've got a gigantic oak in the middle of our front yard. It would be great to grow some fruit trees, but the sunlight is pretty thin..."

"Useless" trees are the ink smudge in the middle of many otherwise pristine gardening plans. I have relatives in Ft. Lauderdale who have multiple amazing live oak trees across their acre of land. The density of the canopy means that it's very hard to add more useful species anywhere in their yard. This is a shame, since South Florida has a year-round gardening climate that can support an incredibly diverse variety of tropical crops such as cinnamon, star fruit, coffee, papaya, black pepper, and jack fruit.

Instead, the yard is filled with oaks. My mother-in-law loves the idea of growing fruit, but not the idea of taking out her mature (and beautiful) unproductive trees.

I think a lot of people fall into that category. It's hard to kick.

After all, cutting down trees is *RealSuperAwfulEvilBad*, as we learned in school, in *The Lord of the Rings*, and in every single kids show on TV.

So, with that in mind, let me provide some options, starting with the simplest first.

Option #1: Cut down your stupid worthless tree(s)

Yes, this is the easiest option. If a tree is hindering your ability to feed yourself, cut it down. Just make sure that it's really a problem first. Mature trees, even non-edible ones, have some benefits we'll get into later. Sometimes it's too easy to fire up the Stihl and go to town. That said, don't be too fearful of taking one out. If you've weighed the options and found your gardening space wanting, do it. Just don't let a tree company take away all the leftover chunks of tree. More on that later in this chapter.

Option #2: Work around your stupid worthless tree(s)

This is another option and often a very good one.

Sometimes having extra shade is a good thing, particularly in climates that have intense summers. By cutting a tree down, will you be turning that space into an oven, unprotected from the blazing sun? Can you use your tree as a shelter for tender plants such as lettuce?

Near where I live there's a farm that intercrops mustard and pecan trees. The mustard plants grow later in the season and can be harvested longer because they're protected by shade. In a sunny location, they'd be gone a lot faster.

Beyond the "sun protection" side of things, there's also the cold to think about. Trees create micro climates that protect plants that are near them from the full force of a freezing night.

Case in point: I once planted two citrus trees. One was beneath the edge of an oak canopy, the other was out in the open. I forgot to cover them one frosty night. The one beneath the oak came through completely unscathed, whereas the other tree froze halfway to the ground.

Micro climates are powerful things. That "worthless" tree may be useful to your yard's environment in ways you don't realize.

Option #3: Let the stupid worthless tree(s) work for you

Trees do a lot of hard work. They add oxygen to the air, release moisture from the soil, help breezes form, and they produce a lot of compostable leaves. Those leaves contain minerals that your tree pulled from deep in the earth, below where your tomatoes and other annuals can reach. When they waft to the ground in the fall, they're feeding and protecting the ground beneath.

Are you raking them up and throwing them away?

Don't. And don't burn them either.

I hate to write that, because I love blazing leaf fires, but they're better when turned into compost.

If you have an oak tree, you can also feed the acorns to livestock, making the combined fall of leaves for the garden and acorns for the animals a pretty good pay-off for just letting that thing sit there.

Option #4: Use the stupid worthless tree(s) as part of a food forest plan

Plants and trees like to live in community. A nice big tree is a shelter for birds, animals, and insects. Start planting smaller edible trees around it and work out from there. The shade, a bit of wind protection, and falling leaves will benefit the young saplings around it, provided they're not too close, all while providing shelter for insect-eating birds and other good guys.

And you know, sometimes you don't really need a "great" reason to leave a tree in place. I left a magnolia tree in my food forest because it was beautiful and because my kids liked to climb it.

In that sense, I suppose it's a habitat for a beneficial organism: *Homo sapiens subsp. "Goodi."*

Though this is by no means a complete list of options, it's a good start. There's really no such thing as a stupid worthless tree. There's a value in any tree. It's up to you to find it.

You may just decide if the value of growing something else is greater than the value of the tree that's in the way. In that case, chop away.

But before you do, let me further defend the beautiful oak trees my mother-in-law loves more than tropical fruit.

Consider one of those oaks. Let's go deeper into what it does. Think about how much work it takes for that tree to grow. It spends its year gathering minerals and water from the soil in her yard (and from the neighbors' yards). Sometimes, the roots of a tree will stretch six times as broad as the canopy of a tree, allowing that tree to pull up nutrients from everywhere. That oak is mining the ground and building its mass with what it finds.

And there's more.

That "worthless" tree is a massive solar collector, capturing sunlight, and converting it into solid oak. What is that solid oak made from? Sugar! Trees are made of cellulose, which is a sugar.

Trees are sugar. Think of that next time you see a tree.

My mother-in-law's oaks are also efficient pumps. They gather many gallons of water from the soil and transpire it into the air through their leaves, planting the seeds of future rainstorms.

An oak also produces gallons of acorns. Pull your car beneath their shade, and you'll hear the rolling crunch of a hundred acorns popping beneath the tires. Acorns feed squirrels, insects, birds, and various mammals. Those creatures leave their droppings behind, feeding the oak in return.

One of my mother-in-law's oaks has a cavity in its side. For years, that cavity has been sporadically occupied by honeybees. Though their honey is inaccessible, their pollination activity has a positive effect on the mangos and other tropical fruit growing nearby, not to mention the vegetable gardens that might be in the neighborhood.

Since my mother-in-law's home is located in the warm subtropics, her oak trees also play host to a wide range of other plant species. For example, they host lichens, fungi, algae, Spanish moss, air plants, climbing cacti, ivy, resurrection ferns, and even native orchids. One oak tree is a complex ecosystem all by itself.

And did you realize that certain mushrooms will only live in combination with certain trees? Porcini, chanterelles, morels, and truffles have their preferred host trees and will often live nowhere else. If you like mushrooms, leave some mature hardwoods, and get yourself a good guide book. There's a patch of oaks about ten miles from my house that I've returned to again and again for baskets of bolete mushrooms.

Free gourmet food.

Beyond the plants and fungi, there are the aforementioned bees, as well as squirrels, bats, owls, birds, anoles, iguanas, snakes, beetles, spiders, and potentially hundreds of other creatures living in a mature live oak.

Those creatures increase the health of the surrounding ecosystem by supplying checks and balances. A patch of mowed grass is a pathetic low-level environment; a mature fern-embroidered oak is a veritable city filled with millions of residents.

What does all this have to do with composting? Perhaps not much; but it should make you think twice about busting out the chain saw. Composting a mature live oak tree should be low on your list. If at all possible, maintaining it as a portion of a greater gardening plan will lead to a richer and healthier environment for everything else you decide to grow. Rather than chop it down, why not plant shade-loving annuals beneath it?

Or build a tree fort. That's always good.

Here's another thought on those trees: what if you considered them as long-term compost factories?

Most trees drop a lot of leaves in the fall. Gather up bags of leaves and use them to feed a compost pile through the winter. Or use them as mulch around your perennials. We used to set aside fifty to one hundred bags of fall leaves every year and use them as the "brown" portion of our compost piles through the rest of the year. Oak leaves take some time to break down but the resulting compost is rich, moist, and long-lasting.

What if a tree falls? Or if you're forced to cut one down because there's simply no space in which to garden?

Don't just burn it or haul it away. You've got a composting bonanza there if you use it correctly.

There's a method of gardening popularized by Sepp Holzer[14] called "Hugelkultur." In hugelkultur, you take limbs, branches, and trunks, make a big mound, then cover it with a layer of soil. Over a period of time the wood rots and fills with moisture, creating a water and nutrient reservoir for the plants growing above. It's like a massive raised bed with a core of wood.

Another thing you can do with the wood is burn it half-way, then spray the embers down with water to make charcoal, also called "biochar." Take that biochar and mix it with manure, urine, compost, or other nutrient-rich or biologically active solutions, and it will become permeated with both nutrition and beneficial bacteria. Turn it into the soil of your garden to create bacterial and fungal bunkers for the good guys.

Trees produce so much potential compost, it even makes sense to leave invasive specimens around, provided you're going to actively manage the system as discussed in the last chapter: if they grow fast, use 'em for chop-n-drop compost.

My dad and I started a food forest in his sandy and infertile south Florida backyard. One weekend we piled up palm tree trunks, branches, logs, hedge trimmings, leaves, grass clippings, and whatever else the neighbors were throwing out. The resulting stack of biomass was probably two feet tall and covered over a hundred square feet. In the middle and around the edges we planted fruit trees and edible perennials. Within a couple of months you could dig into the pile and find rich black soil, worms, and a wide variety of insects working together to rapidly convert that pile of "waste" into rich soil.

The trees have shot towards the sky and are bearing wonderfully a few years later. Periodically we refresh the biomass, taking chunks of felled trees, ficus trimmings, chopped vines, and whatever will rot and throwing them again around the fruit trees.

Don't look at trees as a waste of space or an invasive pain: look at them as fertility factories.

Your garden will thank you.

12. Container Gardening With Compost

So… are you short on space? Short on cash? Short on soil?

Container garden composting solves all three, though probably not in the way you think.

As previously mentioned, it's *hard* to ever get enough compost. Filling up container gardens with finished good stuff would be a waste of compost and likely an exercise in futility. There's a better way to fill up those containers.

Before we jump into that, however, let's look at why you might want to container garden.

Why You Might Want to Container Garden

Growing in the ground takes work. Soils are too sandy, too dry, too wet, too thick, too acid, too rocky, too weedy—you name it. Containers give the gardener complete control of his creation. He can choose the container he wishes and the soil he desires.

Containers help exclude weeds, are easier draining, can be modular and mobile; plus, anything from pots to sacks to bathtubs can be pressed into service. If a gardener is renting his property, container gardens can be moved to a new location when the lease runs out or a move is desired. If you spend a couple of years improving the soil of a garden bed and then move, you've lost that work.

Another benefit of container gardens is that they're easy to turn into self-watering systems. One super-simple way to do this: take a five-gallon bucket and drill small drainage holes about two inches up from the bottom. Fill the bottom with gravel and the rest with potting soil. Water well, and the bottom couple of inches become a reservoir.

Container gardens have their downside, of course. They're usually too small for serious food production. They can also look like a cluttered mess if you're not careful. They may also require you to buy potting soil, since filling them with regular dirt from your backyard usually leads to drainage issues and rotten roots.

Of course, if you have enough biomass available, you can really cut down on the potting soil required.

Filling In the Gaps

If you're interested in container gardening but don't feel like blowing a week's wages on bags of overpriced potting soil, it's time to start some compost-based container gardens.

There's always compostable material lying around that just doesn't fit a fast composting method: items such as chunks of wood, paper plates, sticks, chicken bones, junk mail, etc.

Instead of throwing that in a corner or using it to mulch around trees (junk mail looks really bad blowing around a front yard) or gardens, use it as padding for your container gardens.

How so?

First, get yourself a good-sized container with good drainage. Something like a bathtub, a punctured horse trough, a galvanized tub, or even a stacked cinder block raised bed will work.

Then, start piling up the hard-to-compost materials in the bottom, leaving space for a final layer of potting soil.

Pack in leaves, shredded paper, phone books, torn bedsheets, dead tomato plants, potato peelings, and whatever else you find. Stuff it all in there and smash it down as best as you can. Wet it as you go and keep wetting it until it's sopping. Then cover your compostables with a six-inch layer of loose potting soil. Water that soil well so it fills in the cracks between your original organic matter, then smooth it out and plant away.

Over the years the biomass beneath the surface will rot away and keep feeding your plants.

If you think you've got too much carbon in the bottom, throw in some cottonseed meal, manure, urine, feathers, or even handfuls of dog food before you finish the top layer of soil. That will help things cook. If you want to get really fancy, grab some worms from your worm bin and let them have at it.

I've found that I can grow quite decent container gardens on top of trash that would normally end up in the dump. This method also works in raised beds, though it's not the best for root crops such as carrots, onions, and potatoes, since they tend to get lodged into the rough material beneath the surface. It's also not that nice to turn the soil and accidentally pull up a rotten paperback or beetle-chewed T-shirt. Burying them again is rather a pain, so I stick to this method in long-term perennial beds or container gardens.

Give it a try. Before long you'll be seeing every fallen log and stack of used paper plates as potential container garden stuffers.

13. Composting With Chickens

What if there were a way to magically transform baked beans, worms, carrot peels, grass, and other organic matter directly into nitrogen-rich fertilizer for the garden overnight?

There is!

The magical machine that makes this remarkable transformation is called *Gallus gallus domesticus*, more commonly known as a "chicken."

Though chicken manure is considered to be a very "hot" manure, meaning that it will burn plants if applied fresh and indiscriminately, it can still be used without composting by carefully side-dressing plants or by tilling it into the soil in moderate quantities during the preparation of a garden bed.

If chicken manure is allowed to dry, it can be bagged and stored indefinitely. If it's mixed into a pile of leaves and wet, it will jumpstart the composting process. It can also be mixed with water and used as a liquid fertilizer.

Turning scraps into chicken manure is a sweet way to create treasure from trash. You could call it one of the most direct compost-ing methods possible, even though manure may not be technically "compost." At the very least it's some serious recycling.

Chickens are one of the greatest composting resources in the homesteader's arsenal. Beyond the direct creation of manure, they create eggs and meat, destroy insect pests, till the soil, clear ground, and eat weed seeds.

Chickens are much like pigs in their ability to eat a huge range of foods. They'll eat grass, seeds, frogs, meat, leftover cake, baked beans, watermelon rinds… you name it, they'll probably eat it or try to eat it. They'll even eat other chickens if you give them half a chance.

I recall once slaughtering a bird that had turned mean and sud-denly finding myself surrounded by the rest of the free-range flock, begging for scraps.

That's hard core.

If you're interested in turning scraps into compost, rather than just manure, there are a few ways you can put your birds to work.

The Chicken-Accessible Compost Pile

Instead of turning a compost pile, why not let the chickens do it for you?

Chickens love to hunt and scratch through piles of organic de-bris. If you've ever mulched a fruit tree or a garden and then let your chickens free-range, you know how rapidly they can remove a layer of organic matter. They'll tear and scratch and throw material all over the place in search of worms, insects, and seeds for their ever-hungry gizzards.

If you fence in a compost pile with a short fence that allows your birds to hop into the pile, they'll tear through your compost every time they get a chance. The fence is necessary if you'd like to keep your compost since they'll rapidly scatter it all over a large area if you pile it in an open place.

That said, you will still lose a decent amount of compost because the chickens will consume quite a bit of what you toss in your pile, then later drop it elsewhere as manure. A benefit of this method of composting is that it cuts down on the fly population since the birds will pick out every maggot they find in the pile (along with every roach, beetle, and worm.)

The Rotating Chicken Garden

If you're imagining a spinning chicken, please take a moment to collect yourself.

As farmers and experienced gardeners understand, crop rotation is an important practice for the reduction of pests and diseases in the soil. Adding livestock to a rotation is even better. Chickens are among the best animals for your garden as long as they're not free-ranging through it. They'll eat insects, remove weeds, till the soil, and add manure all at the same time.

To maximize the benefits of chickens, they need to be contained. This requires a "chicken tractor." A chicken tractor is a mobile chicken coop/run that protects the birds from predators while simultaneously protecting the rest of your yard from the chickens.

Since chickens will naturally eat a wide range of grasses and weeds, moving a tractor on a regular basis feeds your birds and fertilizes the land beneath. Famous farmer Joel Salatin has used this to great effect at Polyface Farm[15], though his main emphasis is on growing grass to feed his animals. Whatever you're growing, rotating chickens through the system is usually a big help. In Mr. Salatin's case, he moves the birds at very short intervals to ensure they don't tear up his pastures. In the garden, however, you can put the birds on the weedy remains of last year's garden and let them tear at the dirt until they're on bare ground.

I once had a dream in which I planned out a marvelous set of garden beds matched to a chicken tractor that fit exactly over the top of each bed.

I woke up and drew a sketch of the design.

Imagine this: you create twenty 4' x 8' garden plots and one 4' x 8' chicken tractor. After crops are harvested from a bed, the chickens can be added for a week, clearing the soil and manuring it for the crop to follow. You can leave the remnants of the crops you've harvested right there for the chickens to eat. They'll compost it for you—no bin required.

Food forest guru Geoff Lawton[16] uses simple chicken tractors to open up virgin land before he plants trees in a new food forest. A patch of dense weeds will fall rapidly before the constant picking and scratching of chickens. You can then move the tractor and pop in a few trees, shrubs, or vegetables. Your birds and the soil get fed at the same time.

Harvesting Chicken-Enriched Soil

Another method for using chickens to create compost comes from the aforementioned Paul Gautschi, creator of the "Back to Eden" garden. He keeps chickens in a standard coop with a fenced run, rather than in tractors. To feed them, he throws all his garden scraps over the fence and lets the birds tear through them. Over time, the chickens greatly enrich the soil in their run. There are no weeds or vegetation in their run—nothing but manure-rich fluffy soil, filled with years worth of nutrients that originally traveled in with the scraps and then were devoured, excreted, and turned into the ground by Mr. Gautschi's poultry.

To harvest this fertility, Gautschi took a hardware cloth sifting screen, a wheelbarrow, and a shovel into his chicken run and started digging. The screen allowed him to shake out undecomposed plant debris and stones while filling his wheelbarrow with perfect garden soil that he could use in his garden.

I've pitched lots of seedy weeds, kitchen scraps, leftovers from church dinners, and other tough-to-compost items into my chicken yard. They eat it, turn it in, poop on it, turn it again, and leave behind some really nice dirt. I rarely have weed seeds popping up after the chickens are done, and my crops grow nicely in beds topped off with microbe and nutrient-rich dirt from the chicken run.

It's simple, and it's easy.

If you're already keeping chickens in a run, why not bypass the compost pile and just start digging up the goodness?

What About Ducks?

For the more adventurous homesteader, ducks also present an excellent way to create soil fertility. They have some disadvantages compared to chickens; however, they also provide some benefits that chickens do not.

Unlike chickens, ducks are waterfowl. They need access to some standing water in order to stay happy and healthy. This doesn't have to be a pond, of course. All you really need is a cheap plastic kiddie pool.

A few years ago I kept a small flock of ducks. I placed their kiddie pool "pond" at the base of a young mulberry tree I wanted to grow, figuring that it would appreciate the extra water. What I failed to anticipate was how incredibly filthy ducks are and how much manure they create.

Give them a pool of nice clean water, and they'll muck it up fast. They pig out on feed, scraps, worms, and bugs, then slosh their bills in the water, spilling food into the pond. They eject prodigious quantities of feces into the water and around it. Algae loves this fertility, of course, so if you don't change the water constantly it will turn into a mucky, green scum-filled sludge pond.

Placing that mucky green scum-filled sludge pond at the base of my little mulberry tree was probably the best thing that could have happened for that struggling specimen of *Morus nigra*. The ducks were constantly splashing that filthy (and nutrient-rich) water out all around the tree. Think about it: daily liquid fertilizer right in the root zone. It grew from 18 inches tall to 20 feet in three years. I have never seen a tree grow so fast.

If you have multiple fruit trees, you can rotate your kiddie pool duck pond from tree to tree, and they'll thrive on the attention. The ducks will find water wherever you put it.

As for composting, ducks aren't as good at picking through kitchen scraps as chickens are, but they're pretty close. I find them to be better bug, snail, and slug hunters than chickens. They find food to eat when other birds would starve. All of what they eat gets turned into meat, eggs, and manure. That's a great return. Their best use, in my opinion, is as creators of pools of amazing liquid fertilizer.

If you're not able to let your ducks wander around, you can always place their pond on a high spot and run a hose or a pipe out of the bottom, letting you directly water trees with their mucky, green, scum-filled sludge pond fertilizer. If you'd like to get your exercise, you can just fill watering cans with the water from the duck run and then water your plants by hand.

Whatever you do, it's going to work.

Chickens and ducks, even if they don't produce eggs or meat, are composting maestros. Add them to your homesteading plans, and your plants will thank you with abundant harvests and luxuriant growth.

14. Stretching Your Compost

Dave's #1 Inarguable Rule of Composting: *No matter how much compost you make, you'll never have as much as you want.*

The breakdown of organic matter into well-done compost yields remarkably little finished product.

It's very, very sad.

I'm concluding this book with this chapter because you need to know there's hope for your gardens even if your compost yields are low.

Organic gardeners often use massive amounts of compost in their plots.

"Square-Foot Gardening," for example, recommends creating soil for your beds that consist of 1/3 finished compost.[17]

That is a *lot* of compost to make yourself. It's also expensive to buy if you're doing more than just a bed or two.

The fact is: compost is amazing stuff. It doesn't need to be added in huge quantities to keep your gardens healthy or your plants strong.

This is good, because of **Dave's #1 Inarguable Rule of Composting.**

Here's how a gardener can stretch his compost and keep the garden happy without spending twenty-eight hours a day building and turning piles.

The answer is only seven words long:

Compost Tea in a Big Stinky Barrel

A couple of years ago I planted a large (for me) plot of field corn in a sandy, freshly plowed field. Since it was way too much space to be improved by adding compost (the truckload required would have cost way more than the corn I hoped to harvest), I put a couple shovelfuls of chicken manure into the bottom of a 55 gallon drum, then filled it two-thirds full of water.

Every time I visited my field (about every two weeks or so) I'd stir the amazing smelling slop in the barrel and then fill a couple of cheap watering cans (with the roses removed) and walk along the corn rows, letting the manure/compost water stream out at the base of the stalks. The corn responded excellently, growing at a remarkable rate, and keeping a rich green color throughout the season. I stretched two shovelfuls of manure across 2500 square feet of corn!

If I had added that chicken manure to my compost pile, then tried to spread compost down the rows, it wouldn't have made a dent in the fertility of the soil. There simply would not have been enough compost.

Along with the manure, I also added a bit of Epsom salts for magnesium, plus a few cups of fish emulsion and liquid seaweed fertilizer. Though the main thing corn "eats" is nitrogen, I have a gut feeling that adding lots of micro nutrients promotes stronger growth. Unlike many manure or compost "tea" makers, I don't bother aerating the stuff.

Last fall, I filled a trash can with pulled weeds, leaves, some chicken manure, straw, and a bit of dirt, then filled it the rest of the way with water, and let it rot for a while. I then dipped into that water and fed my plants in the greenhouse throughout the winter. They did quite well, though the smell—my gosh—was amazing. (I think I need to market it: Dave's Fetid Swamp Water™).

Incidentally, you're supposed to keep air in the mix in order to encourage the friendly and less dangerous aerobic bacteria, but hey, who can fault a guy for sending a little love over to the anaerobic side once in a while? I've thrown in yogurt, kefir, molasses, urine, compost, comfrey leaves, stale coffee, leftover water from cooking beans and greens, ashes, and a tablespoon of borax for boron.

The satisfying part of weed tea is that you're taking "waste" and converting it into an asset.

Weeds are great at accumulating nutrients from the soil. That's what makes them such hardy competitors in the garden. Take their hard work, and make it work for you.

Urine is another great addition to compost teas. As I mentioned in chapter 7, I've seen an amazing garden fed with nothing but diluted urine, so I know this method works. It also makes sense if you consider the order inherent in the universe. If I were going to design a system, I would make the waste from one organism feed another.

As mentioned previously, urine is sterile when it leaves the human body, so you're not dealing with questions such as, "Will this kill me?"

Urine has an NPK rating of roughly 15-1-2 which is comparable to commercial nitrogen fertilizers.

You can also make compost tea from just compost. Take an old T-shirt or fine mesh bag, and fill it with good compost, then submerge it in a bucket of water for a day or more, swishing it around as you remember. The resulting "tea" is loaded with beneficial bacteria, fungi, minerals, and other good stuff. I don't usually make straight compost tea, since I like to add more fertilization to the mix with the ingredients mentioned above. However, compost tea is great as a spray for treating fungal issues on plants.

NOTE: There are methods of anaerobic compost tea creation that rely on purchased mixes of bacteria. Some folks swear by these, and they may have some merit. As for me, I've done quite well simply throwing in a wide mix of manure, compost, etc., and then letting the local microorganisms have at it.

The big problem with making manure/compost tea as I do is that it's not safe to directly consume. There can be some bad guys hanging around in that mix, so a gardener should avoid this method of fertilization on his patches of salad greens and other plants that are eaten raw unless he's prepared to thoroughly wash everything.

I've never gotten sick; however, I usually use this type of mix on plants such as corn, fruit trees, young seedlings, and greenhouse plants that aren't going to be directly consumed or harvested within a short period after fertilization.

The barrel method is my favorite way to stretch compost out over a lot of square footage and it's so easy to do you'll be a convert once you start.

Tiny Bits of Compost

Unlike what you've been told, plants don't require massive amounts of organic matter in order to be happy. The levels of humus in healthy native soils are usually only at a few percent, and that's enough for most crops. Adding living compost to the soil inoculates your plants with a wide variety of microorganisms and fungi. It definitely should be added; it just doesn't need to be piled on.

In some situations, such as in sandy soils, keeping high levels of compost in the ground is a losing proposition. In those cases, mulching on top with decaying organic matter makes more sense than mixing in lots of compost when you plant.

I've seen compost stirred into the garden soil of a small plot in the hot sand of south Florida with nary a trace to be seen a few months later. It leaches out, blows away, and is consumed by the relentless microscopic denizens of the subtropics.

Of course, mulch makes a huge difference in that case. It becomes compost and is pulled down into the plants' root zones by worms and other creatures, taking a while to compost and a little longer to disappear. When you plant in a situation like that, just add a little finished compost around your seedlings, top off with some mulch, and then water well. That will save you a lot of work and wasted humus.

Compost is also very useful for seed germination, although you should make sure you have fine stuff. A compost sifter is quite handy to have and takes only a few minutes to construct.

To make one, just construct a square or rectangular frame of two by fours, then staple half-inch hardware cloth to it. I have a little twelve-inch frame for small compost jobs, plus another one that's about 18" x 36" and sits on top of my wheelbarrow for some serious sifting. Sifted compost can be bagged and saved for future potting and transplanting projects. It often makes sense for the gardener to sift and sort compost before he needs it; this keeps him from having to break his stride while working on a larger garden project.

When new beds are pressed into production, seeds can be planted in indentations created with the handle of a hoe laid on the ground and gently stepped upon. Sprinkle compost over the seeds, then water it in.

You can also add a half-inch or so of compost to the top of a new bed and rake or till it in. It works, even in small amounts. Water that bed through the growing season with compost tea, and your plants will be very happy.

If you're really feeling lazy about compost creation or still don't have enough, you can just take your new sifter into a local patch of woods and rake up some of the forest duff and sift it into buckets. That's some rich and fungi-filled material. It's especially good compost for using around young trees and shrubs since it contains many of the organisms they need.

Compost shortages will happen, but they don't have to spell the end for your garden. Barrels of tea and spot applications will get you through without a bump.

Epilogue

We live inside a marvelously designed ecosystem that's also a remarkable recycling machine. Making that machine work for you and your plants takes a little thought, but it will save you lots of money and resources in the long term while enriching your little piece of the planet.

I hope the previous pages have sparked some good ideas. Gardening and composting don't have to be the precise and rule-bound processes local extension services might have you believe. If you get inspired to start saving logs from the burn pile and fish guts from the dumpster, I've done my job, and I salute you, fellow scavenger of long-term fertility!

For daily gardening inspiration and insight, please visit my daily gardening blog at www.floridasurvivalgardening.com.

For rare edible perennials, you can also check out my nursery at www.floridafoodforests.com.

I'd like to thank my friend Jeanne Logue for her proofreading and excellent notations on this book. I'd also like to thank another wonderful gal that proofread for me but refused to let me give her credit. You know who you are.

A big thanks are also in order to Chet and Dave Womach of ThePrepperProject.com for graciously allowing me to reuse portions of my online columns in this book. Their generosity helped make this publication possible and I recommend checking out their site.

Thanks to JartStar for the fantastic cover to this book. I had a simple idea—he made it look great.

Finally, I'm honored to have been published by my friend and editor Vox Day along with his team at Castalia House.

Now get thee outside and compost!

David The Good
Ocala, Florida
2015

Notes

[1] Ruth Stout, *Gardening Without Work: For the Aging, the Busy & the Indolent* (Norton Creek Press, 2011 [reworked and reprinted edition]). Ruth's approach to gardening basically boiled down to mulch, mulch, mulch, mulch, mulch, and more mulch. She has a wry wit and a sparkling personality that draws in readers. Worth checking out, particularly if you like mulch. Lots of mulch.

[2] Patricia Lanza, *Lasagna Gardening: A New Layering System for Bountiful Gardens: No Digging, No Tilling, No Weeding, No Kidding* (Rodale Books; English Language edition, 1998). I confess, I haven't read this book; however I have heard an interview with the author and found her to be engaging. For those interested in the deep mulch method, this book is well-rated.

[3] Dana Richardson & Sarah Zentz, *Back to Eden*, 2011 (http://www.backtoedenfilm.com). Starring farmer Paul Gautschi, the film *Back to Eden* is an encouraging look at how one man transformed a patch of rock-hard clay into a rich vegetable garden and orchard through the application of prodigious

quantities of mulch, compost, and faith. Available to watch online at the website or via purchase as a DVD. I bought and recommend the film.

[4] Mart Hale is one of those guys with a mind like a computer. I met him a few years ago, and we quickly became friends. From biomass stoves to tilapia, food forests to mushroom cultivation, the man is a mad scientist of homesteading. Check out his YouTube channel here: http://www.youtube.com/user/marthale7.

[5] Larry Grim is another one of those guys who does everything. He's built some impressive chicken tractors, pluckers, and brooders, installed solar lighting, made bows from PVC, and he installs whole home vacuum systems. If you live in central Florida and want a vacuum system, his site is http://pcvacs.com/.

[6] Mary Appelhof, *Worms Eat My Garbage* (Flower Press; Revised and expanded second edition, 2003). This is the premier starter book on vermicomposting.

[7] Steve Solomon, *Gardening When It Counts: Growing Food in Hard Times* (New Society Publishers, 2006). This book is a must-have for preppers and serious gardeners. Go buy it.

[8] John Starnes is a gardener/farmer living in the Tampa area. His blog can be found at http://www.johnstarnesurbanfarm.blogspot.com/.

[9] Pat Frank, *Alas, Babylon* (J. B. Lippincott, 1959). Still an

excellent read for its compelling and realistic look at a post-nuclear apocalypse scenario.

[10] Joseph Jenkins, *The Humanure Handbook* (Joseph Jenkins, Inc., 3rd edition, 2005.) A must-own for anyone even vaguely interested in composting human "waste" or living off grid.

[11] Jenkins does urge readers not to overlook the potential dangers of raw sewage; however, he also firmly believes in the ability of nature to recycle human "waste" into soil, provided it is given the chance.

[12] Jenkins relates, "It is estimated that one person's annual urine output contains enough soil nutrients to grow grain to feed that person for a year." Jenkins takes this estimate from a Swedish publication titled "Ecological Sanitation," p. 75, published by the Swedish International Development Cooperation Agency in 1998, editor Uno Winblad.

[13] John Jeavons, *How to Grow More Vegetables* (8th edition, Ten Speed Press, 2012.)

[14] Sepp Holzer, known as the Rebel Farmer, is a great giant of an Austrian who has created a garden paradise in the inhospitable wind-swept pines of the Alps. I highly recommend his book *Sepp Holzer's Permaculture*, along with anything else he writes. His creation of microclimates, hugelkultur gardens, polycultures, plant breeding programs, and fruit tree experimentation are legendary.

[15] Polyface Farm is an impressive operation. Their website is http://www.polyfacefarms.com/.

[16] To see the single most inspiring film you'll find on food forests, check out Geoff Lawton's movie *Establish a Food Forest the Permaculture Way*. It's a paradigm-shifting presentation.

[17] Mel Bartholomew, *All New Square Foot Gardening* (First printing revised edition, Cool Springs Press, 2005). Though I pick on the amount of compost used in Bartholomew's gardening method, there's no denying that "square foot gardening" is incredibly popular. I've had mixed results with it; however, Mel Bartholomew has probably launched more new gardeners than any other writer.

CPSIA information can be obtained at www.ICGtesting.com
Printed in the USA
LVOW07s0500271115

464318LV00015B/482/P

9 789527 065563